More Praise for *The Female Vision*

"*The Female Vision* provides an essential guidebook for leaders of the future. Those seeking to inspire and engage women's talents will find it indispensable."

—Frances Hesselbein, Distinguished Chair of
Leadership, US Military Academy, West Point, and
recipient of the Presidential Medal of Freedom

"The book deserves our full attention! The authors make a compelling case for why we need to rethink leadership development and selection. They show why we desperately need leaders who exhibit broad-spectrum notice, find satisfaction in the daily experience of work, and have a penchant for viewing work in a larger social context."

—Linda A. Hill, Wallace Brett Donham Professor
of Business Administration and Faculty Chair,
The Leadership Initiative, Harvard Business School

"Nothing has more potential for healing the planet than the purposeful vision of women. This book paves the way!"

—Richard Leider, author of *The Power of Purpose*

"The world is experiencing a crisis of confidence about its leaders. *The Female Vision* shows how women can address this by redefining leadership. It's the right message for women and for girls!"

—Kathy Cloninger, CEO, Girl Scouts of the USA

"*The Female Vision* is essential for those who want to understand the real difference women's leadership can make to our economy and society by emphasizing the power of women's strategic thinking."

—Linda Basch, President, National Council for Research on Women

"*The Female Vision* digs deep to find ˌˌˌˌˌˌˌˌˌ ˌˌˌˌˌˌˌ ˌˌˌˌˌ progress has stalled and shows why companies believe it, live it!"

—Margar

"Women leaders are underrepresented ˌˌˌˌ, ˌˌˌˌˌˌˌ is well as in the corporate world. *The Female Vision* clearly articulates ˌˌˌat women uniquely bring to leadership of any organization."

—Susan E. Danish, Executive Director,
Association of Junior Leagues International

"The economic crisis provided a wake-up call. Organizations must do a better job of drawing on women's visionary talents. Thank you, Sally and Julie, for building the case!"

—Jacki Zehner, former partner, Goldman Sachs, and Vice-Chair, Women's Funding Network

"Sally Helgesen and Julie Johnson show the price the world pays for not listening to women but also shows women what they must do to be heard."

—Michelle Clayman, founder and Chair, Clayman Institute for Gender Research, Stanford University

"Visionary! Twenty-first century leadership, talent, and market imperatives make this book a mandatory management read. A real eye-opener."

—Avivah Wittenberg-Cox, author of *How Women Mean Business*

"The business case has been proven—financial results are far better with women in the C-suite and the boardroom. Sally and Julie's research shows CEOs how to set a new tone at the top by leveraging the competitive advantage of women's leadership."

—Janice Reals Ellig, Co-CEO, Chadick Ellig Executive Search Advisors, and President, New York Women's Forum

"Provocative and timely. *The Female Vision* shows why what women see *matters*. It offers strategies for women seeking to develop their leadership capacity and actionable advice for employers to help them do so."

—Mary Brabeck, Dean, Steinhardt School of Culture, Education, and Human Development, New York University

"Too much male-think brought the world's financial system to its knees. It's time to bring *The Female Vision* into the corner office!"

—Consuelo Mack, anchor and Managing Editor, *WealthTrack*

"Reading *The Female Vision* can help women assume greater control. As I read it, I kept thinking, 'This is how I really think, feel, and work.'"

—Michele Coleman Mayes, Senior Vice President and General Counsel, Allstate

The
female
VISION

BOOKS BY SALLY HELGESEN

The Female Advantage: Women's Ways of Leadership

The Web of Inclusion: A New Architecture for Building Great Organizations

Thriving in 24/7: Six Strategies for Taming the New World of Work

Everyday Revolutionaries: Working Women and the Transformation of American Life

Wildcatters: A Story of Texans, Oil, and Money

The
female
VISION

Women's Real Power at Work

SALLY HELGESEN *&* JULIE JOHNSON

BK

Berrett–Koehler Publishers, Inc.
San Francisco
a BK Life book

Berrett-Koehler Publishers, Inc.
1333 Broadway, Suite 1000
Oakland, CA 94612-1921
Tel: (510) 817-2277   Fax: (510) 817-2278   www.bkconnection.com

Ordering Information

Quantity sales. Special discounts are available on quantity purchases by corporations, associations, and others. For details, contact the "Special Sales Department" at the Berrett-Koehler address above.

Individual sales. Berrett-Koehler publications are available through most bookstores. They can also be ordered directly from Berrett-Koehler: Tel: (800) 929-2929; Fax: (802) 864-7626; www.bkconnection.com

Orders for college textbook/course adoption use. Please contact Berrett-Koehler: Tel: (800) 929-2929; Fax: (802) 864-7626.

Orders by U.S. trade bookstores and wholesalers. Please contact Ingram Publisher Services, Tel: (800) 509-4887; Fax: (800) 838-1149; E-mail: customer.service@ ingrampublisherservices.com; or visit www.ingrampublisherservices.com/Ordering for details about electronic ordering.

Berrett-Koehler and the BK logo are registered trademarks of Berrett-Koehler Publishers, Inc.

Printed in the United States of America

Berrett-Koehler books are printed on long-lasting acid-free paper. When it is available, we choose paper that has been manufactured by environmentally responsible processes. These may include using trees grown in sustainable forests, incorporating recycled paper, minimizing chlorine in bleaching, or recycling the energy produced at the paper mill.

Library of Congress Cataloging-in-Publication Data

Helgesen, Sally, 1948–
   The female vision : women's real power at work / Sally Helgesen and Julie Johnson. — 1st ed.
      p.   cm.
  Includes bibliographical references and index.
  ISBN 978-1-57675-382-8 (alk. paper)
   1. Women in the professions. 2. Women executives. 3. Leadership. I. Johnson, Julie. II. Title.
  HD6054.H45   2010
  331.4—dc22   2010006690

First Edition

20 19 18 17 16 15   10 9 8 7 6 5

Cover Design: Karen Marquardt
Cover Photo: Anthony Loew
Interior designed and produced by BookMatters; copyedited by Katie Silver; proofread by Tanya Grove; indexed by Gerald Van Ravenswaay.

For Our Mothers:

Ann LaFollette Helgesen
&
Verna Ione Johnson

CONTENTS

FOREWORD

Marshall Goldsmith

"I decided it just wasn't worth it."

Too many gifted women have used this phrase to describe why they departed from major corporations and passed up seemingly spectacular career opportunities, leaving positions that may have seemed glamorous to the outside observer but that felt personally depleting to them. I hope the wisdom and insights the authors share in *The Female Vision* will change that situation by giving organizations a way to draw more fully on what women see.

The Female Vision draws on the latest research (comparing women's and men's perceptions) to illustrate *why* what women and men see can be so different. It presents myriad examples from today's challenging workplace to illustrate why these differences matter and how women's vision can make a significant, positive difference in the workplace.

Even more importantly, the authors provide practical suggestions that can help women increase the probability that their vision is not only recognized but also implemented in organizations. *The Female Vision* also provides organizations with guidelines on how to incorporate women's best observations into strategy and culture, building a comprehensive and inclusive vision for the company's future.

Most of the problems that led to the recent economic meltdown occurred in organizations dominated by men. These organizations illustrated classic stereotypical "male" behaviors, such as focusing on short-term profitability, a preoccupation with "making the numbers," and a devotion to short-term personal—rather than long-term corporate—wealth. Who knows? Perhaps organizations that embraced more women in strategic roles and recognized their broader vision would not have experienced the same degree of crisis. We all would have been better off!

The Female Vision represents the collaborative effort of two wonderful professionals, who are also good friends of mine, Sally Helgesen and Julie Johnson. The breadth and depth of knowledge and the years of experience that Sally and Julie bring to the party shine through the pages of this book. Sally's background in research and journalism is evident in the clarity and richness of the writing. She is a gifted interviewer and author who can weave insights from multiple sources—survey research, expert opinion, executive interviews, and personal experience—into a coherent and meaningful story. Julie is one of America's most experienced and respected executive coaches. She understands from the inside how senior female executives experience their work and has insights into what corporations can do to incorporate women's vision. She also knows what men are doing right—and what they need to change.

I believe that leaders at all levels, men and women, can benefit from reading *The Female Vision*. Men can benefit by seeing the world from a female perspective that shows why "different" doesn't have to mean "better." Women can benefit by learning how their personal experiences compare with those of other successful women and by gaining new tools to help them make a greater positive difference in the world.

As Sally and Julie aptly illustrate, the problems women face in organizations are rarely the result of male leaders being deliberately mean, callous, or indifferent. Most leaders want to do what's right, for women and for their organizations; they are less sure of how to leverage women's best skills. This book provides several examples of women's leadership programs that have good intentions, but not good results.

Writing this book took courage. Dealing with gender differences (no matter how sensitive the authors try to be) can always be controversial. My suggestion for you, the reader, is simple: Read this book with an open mind. Don't focus on what you disagree with or what you cannot change. Focus on what you agree with and what you can change.

With that in mind, I believe that *The Female Vision* can help both individuals and organizations create a more positive, inclusive, and effective future.

PREFACE

We believe that what women see—what they notice and value and how they perceive the world in operation—is a great underexploited resource in organizations. In this book, we explore what the female vision is, what it has to offer, and why it matters—to women, to organizations, and to the world.

Each of us has worked with women around the world for over twenty years. Sally is an author, speaker, and consultant; Julie has coached hundreds of senior executives in global companies and held leadership positions within major organizations. Our experiences have convinced us that, although women's capacity for vision is profound, companies routinely fail to recognize the power of what women see. As a result, women lose confidence in their own ability to articulate and communicate what they notice, and organizations lose the insights and balance that a female perspective might bring.

Organizations today are far more committed to developing women's talents and leadership potential than in the past, and good companies recognize the value of workforce diversity. Yet women still have limited impact at the strategic level because they are not perceived as visionary.[1] We believe this perception not only gets things wrong, but gets things exactly backward. Women's greatest asset lies in their visionary power.

We came to this belief after four years of research and thinking about the true value that women bring to work. What we present evolved over the course of a long-running conversation that began in 2005 on a beach in La Jolla, California, where we were attending a professional retreat. At the time, each of us was preoccupied with the questions then engaging most people in our field: Why were so many talented women either leaving senior positions or watching their careers stall out? Why weren't more women represented at the senior executive level? Why did major corporate boards do such a poor job of recruiting senior women? We had followed the research and were familiar with phenomena such as the widely discussed "female brain drain." But our own experiences suggested that fundamental issues were not being addressed.

Our conversation kept returning to a phrase that each of us had heard from women who had either left high positions or considered doing so: *I decided it just wasn't worth it.* We realized we could not meaningfully explore the relationship between women and power unless we addressed the question of what women most deeply value and how this might conflict with what mainstream organizations expect their leaders to value.

We began interviewing dozens of senior women and immersing ourselves in academic research on the subject. Our aim was to put together a book that would set what was happening with women in the larger context of values. We soon recognized that we needed to develop original data if we were to accurately describe the values women bring with them to work. We launched a full-scale research study, supported by an association with the National Council for Research on Women and with financial backing from sponsors who saw value in our project. In the final phase of our research, we decided to broaden our perspective and look at the connection between the values women bring to organizations and the vision most women hold about what life and work—at its best—could be.

This book is organized into three sections. In the first, we define the female vision, show why it is important, and describe the consequences of it being undervalued. In the second, we explore the three components that shape the female vision: the capacity for broad-spectrum notice, the ability to find satisfaction in the daily experience of work, and the penchant for viewing work in a larger social context. In the last section, we show how women can act upon their vision and what organizations can do to support them.

We intend this book for a broad audience. We want to engage individual women seeking to identify and articulate their own strengths in order to create more rewarding ways of working and living. We want to help organizations and institutions seeking to develop women leaders and benefit from their strategic strengths. And we want to provide a resource for teachers and students—in colleges and universities and in high schools as well—who hope to build a better world by preparing young women to exercise their vision and develop the leadership skills that will be required in the years ahead.

PART I

Value of the Female Vision

CHAPTER ONE

What Women See

What we notice, what we believe is important, and what we perceive life should be are the primary components that shape our vision. The more authentically we understand, express, and act on the distinctive aspects of what we see, the greater our contribution will be and the more we'll fulfill our purpose in the world.

Translating vision into practice is challenging for anyone, but it can be especially difficult for women in organizations. This is because what women see can be out of sync with what the workplace expects. Having entered the workplace in significant numbers and having begun to assume positions of authority and influence only in the last thirty years, women have had little opportunity to shape the culture of work—its values, assumptions, and expectations.

The disconnect between what organizations expect and what women at their best have to offer has become an issue as workplace demands have grown more intense. Companies today require more from their people—more time, greater commitment, fresher ideas, a continual learning curve. Thriving in this environment requires passion and engagement. But it's difficult to feel fully engaged when your vision, your fundamental way of seeing things, is not understood, recognized, or valued. And it's tough to feel passionate when you feel unable to bring what is best about yourself to your work.

When women's ways of seeing are not validated, it shortchanges women, requiring them to exercise their skills without drawing on the full power of what they notice and value. Operating at less than full capacity undermines their effectiveness and their ability to feel authentic, as well as keeping them from being fully present in the moment. It can also leach away the zestfulness and fun that comes from engaging what is best within themselves and putting that forth into the world.

When women's ways of seeing are not validated, it also shortchanges their organizations, narrowing the base of talents and ideas from which they can draw. In a global environment where change is constant, companies need to be nimble, innovative, and very smart, which is why relying on the usual suspects to do the usual things in the usual way is no longer effective. When organizations fail to appreciate the fullness and scope of what women have to offer, they diminish their capacity to "think outside the box"—a frequently stated objective—because the blinders they require their people to wear keep them firmly inside it.

We've all seen what happens when women's ways of seeing are not recognized or are dismissed as being beside the point. The consequences play out on a large scale—which we'll explore later—and in the smallest interactions.

For example, Jim and Jill are walking out of a sales meeting in which the regional manager has been outlining the sales figures he expects their team to meet in the next quarter. As they step into the hall, Jim, who was scribbling down numbers during the presentation, says, "I figure it's doable if we can get client X to expand his budget by 6 percent while cutting our costs by \$3.2 million."

Jill nods. "That sounds about right. But did you notice how Ron in the back of the room seemed depressed? He's usually so outgoing and engaged."

Jim doesn't respond. He's wondering why Jill is making an irrelevant comment. She needs to be thinking about how they can make their numbers, not worrying about what someone else is feeling. Besides, Jim wasn't looking at Ron. For one thing, he doesn't have eyes in the back of his head. Plus, he was focused on the presentation, which is exactly what the regional manager would expect.

Jill was paying attention, too, but not in a single-minded way. For example, she was aware that some of the attendees couldn't hear what the presenter was saying—not surprising since he has a habit of speaking too fast and then getting testy when someone asks him to repeat his remarks. But it was Ron's disinterest that most caught her attention. He's key to the team's effort, and it's going to be a rough road for everyone if he's struggling.

Still, it's clear to Jill that Jim doesn't want to pursue the subject. She's not sure she can make him understand that she was engaged by the presentation but was also taking in a lot of other things. She also wants to signal to him that she's on board. So she says simply, "I think your numbers are right on target."

This brief exchange typifies a fundamental dynamic that occurs thousands of time every day in the workplace. Both Jim and Jill are bringing useful information to their encounter: Jim by proposing specifics that could move the team ahead, Jill by noting a potential problem that could undermine it. Both Jim's focus and Jill's active antenna offer clear benefits to their sales team.

However, Jim can't see the value in what Jill is trying to contribute, nor has Jill framed her observations in a way that compels Jim's interest. Once Jill senses his skepticism, she backs off rather than persisting in trying to make her case. She gives up on trying to help Jim understand what she sees and tries to placate him instead. As a result, the team misses out on potentially vital information. And Jill winds up ignoring her own best insights, thereby undermining the value she could otherwise bring to the effort.

Such incidents occur because what Jill notices, believes is important, and perceives her company should be—the components of her vision—are to a large extent countercultural in her organization. Sure, the senior executives talk a lot about how "our people are our most important asset." They even had the phrase printed up as a "vision statement" on a laminated card. But it's not their authentic vision because it doesn't reflect what they actually notice or value or how they operate. It's just something the president's speechwriter thought would sound good.

Jim accepts the discrepancy between what the company says and how it acts, and forges ahead. But Jill can't help wishing the company would match its actions to its words. If it did, she'd feel more at home and would have more to contribute. The company would also be a better place to work and would probably have better relationships with clients as a result.

But there's another reason that Jill's observations are not particularly valued in her organization, and that has to do with numbers. Most of what she notices, values, and would like to see can't be easily quantified or expressed by an equation. Many of her perceptions are relatively subjective. By contrast, Jim and the regional division head pride themselves on sticking to what the numbers tell them. The sales VP whom they report to is known for cutting discussions short with a brusque, "Just get to the bottom line." This reflects the company's presumption that numbers are not only an essential business tool but the final determinant of value.

Jill was a math whiz in college, and she can tote up a spreadsheet with the best of them. But she's never believed that numbers tell the whole story. She can't deliver an algorithm to prove that Ron is in a fragile state or offer a figure that quantifies how much his distraction could cost the sales team. Unable to put what she notices in a numerical frame, she can't figure out how to advocate for the value of her observations—so she ends up backing off entirely. She stuffs what she sees, and as a result her interaction with Jim is less authentic and productive than it otherwise might be.

Dr. Mary O'Malley, a neuroscientist and psychiatrist who works with senior executive women, sees exchanges such as the one between Jill and Jim all the time.[1] She notes that women often have difficulty defending the value of what they see in part because the traditional workplace is not necessarily structured to recognize subjective observation. Lacking support, women are likely to lose confidence in the value of what they have to offer and may internalize their inability to do so as a failure. Suppressing their best insights also makes women feel out of place and lowers the quality and authenticity of their exchanges. In the end, everybody loses.

Of course, not all women are like Jill, nor are all men like Jim. We're all individuals whose talents and aptitudes fall along a spectrum. Some women are totally focused on the bottom line and some men exhibit sensitivity to the nuances of human interaction. Some women do not question organizational values and commitments, and some men most certainly do.

But, *in general*, women's observational style tends to be broad and wide-ranging, while men tend to focus more narrowly on what they perceive as relevant to the task at hand. Women are continually scanning their environment for information, whereas men are more apt to restrict their observations to what a specific set of actions requires.[2] These complementary capabilities *should* be a source of strength and offer a perfect demonstration of the benefits that diversity can bring to organizations.

But because diversity is often viewed as a numbers game— "We will increase our percentage of women at director level by 30 percent over the next five years"—companies often end up missing the larger picture. Diversity does not result simply from creating a richer demographic mix. True diversity is the diversity of *values*.[3]

A Brief History of Attention

A physicist might describe the difference between men's and women's ways of seeing by saying that women's attention operates like radar, picking up signals across a wide spectrum, whereas men's attention operates like a laser, focusing on a single point in depth. Attention is the key word here, for what we see is determined by where we direct our attention. Our attention in turn is shaped by how we are accustomed to engaging our senses in the exercise of habitual skills. If we repair cars, we recognize the sound of a faulty belt as soon as the engine engages; if we bake bread, we can tell when a rising loaf is ready for the oven by pressing a finger to its surface. Our skills and experience channel our attention.

Given that men and women have until very recently exercised very different skills in the world, it's hardly surprising that they would—again, *in general*—attend to different things and have different ways of assigning value. Anthropologists like Helen Fisher believe the difference goes all the way back to the earliest phases of human history, when men contributed to their tribe's survival with their hunting prowess while women sustained the group by gathering plants.[4] Clearly, the ability to focus attention on a single task is an advantage when pursuing antelope across the plains, whereas reading the environment broadly is useful when your job is to choose which roots are safe and nourishing while also caring for babies and raising children.

As people settled into small communities, men and women continued to exercise different skills, with men protecting the group and women doing pretty much everything else. As agriculture grew more complex, the division of labor continued, with men working the fields and women tending to house and garden. When work became centralized in the industrial era, men moved from farms into factories and offices while women stayed at home to do the domestic work. With few exceptions, women who did work outside the home were driven by fierce financial necessity. Poorly paid, undereducated, and excluded from leadership positions, they didn't play much of a role in shaping the culture of the industrial workplace.

But the divide that has separated men and women since the dawn of civilization began to erode during the last thirty or forty years, as women entered the workplace in significant numbers and closed the historic education gap with men. This in turn has resulted in men taking a far more active role in raising children and has changed our perception of what it means to be a father. Men and women now exercise many of the same skills in the course of their everyday lives and share more aspects of their daily experience. This erosion of separate spheres has gained speed over the last twenty years as cheap, powerful, networked technologies have decentralized the workplace and begun to transform how both men and women work and live.

The tools we use determine the skills we develop, giving order to our experience and providing us with an identity in the world. The spear, the helmet, and the plow are ancient symbols of male activity, while the infant, the spade, and the spinning wheel have from earliest times symbolized the work of women. This identification of tool with gender persisted well into the industrial era; when Sally graduated from high school, for example, she was given a gold typewriter charm for her bracelet, a symbol that she intended to become a "career girl."

But the advent of the personal computer ended the identification of tool with gender, signaling a major shift in the relationship between men and women. For the first time in human history, men and women are not only using the same primary tool in their work but are also using different iterations of that tool to manage their personal and domestic lives. This requires them to develop similar skills and to use a common language, making our daily experience more similar to each others' than in the past.[5]

As the tissue and the texture of men's and women's lives become more similar, our ways of being in the world become less tied to and determined by gender. Yet we retain fundamental distinctions that are a legacy of our different but complementary histories, for evolution proceeds at a slower pace than technological or social change. One of the most important of these distinctions is the difference in how men and women direct their attention, which in turn determines what we see.

We bring our individual ways of seeing with us to our daily work. The diversity of our perceptions has the potential to broaden and enrich the scope of how organizations make decisions and form connections in the marketplace, but all too often this does not occur. Despite an often sincerely stated commitment to supporting and developing women's talent, many organizations still do not know how to value women's ways of seeing or understand how to use women's insights to their advantage.

The costs to organizations of this failure are not easily quantifiable, but they are very real. The costs to women are more obvious. When women's most authentic observations are not valued, they either resign themselves to suppressing their best contributions, or they decide to take their insights and talents elsewhere. In either case, their capacity as leaders is diminished.

Acting on What We See

We make our vision tangible by acting on what we see. Our actions provide the link between what we see and what we achieve in the world. When we don't have the opportunity to act on our perceptions, our true potential to contribute remains locked inside ourselves. What should be a source of power in the world becomes a source of frustration. This damages our ability to bring our whole self to our tasks and sets us up to feel inauthentic even when we are doing our jobs. Because our minds are divided, we can't be fully ourselves.

Dr. O'Malley believes that the disconnect between what women see and what their organizations value may be the primary reason that women are more likely than men to report feeling fraudulent at work.[6] Elizabeth, a top editor at a major financial magazine, provides a perfect example.

> My boss and colleagues always said I was doing a good job, but I never felt I was because I wasn't able to bring my best thinking to my work. In the morning when I got dressed, I'd look in the mirror and I couldn't put together what I saw with who I was supposed to be. The only thing that made my job feel real was picking up my briefcase. I'd walk out the door with it and think: I *must* be this person because otherwise I wouldn't be carrying this briefcase.

When women like Elizabeth—talented, highly educated, and insightful—feel disconnected from who they think they are supposed to be at work, they can lose energy and a sense of purpose.[7] They also lose touch with the creativity that is available to all of us when we are fully present and engaged—the creativity that is synonymous with *flow*.[8] By routinely suppressing their own best insights, women undermine their own capacity for satisfaction and joy.

Dr. O'Malley observes that people feel fraudulent in situations where their real value is not being acknowledged or in which they are being measured according to a standard that doesn't apply.[9] She says, "It's this vague feeling of unease that occurs when we know we have something real to offer but we don't have the right words to articulate it. When this happens, we tend to measure our self-worth by externalities that always leave us falling short of the mark."

Timothy Keller, the author and pastor, expands upon this observation. He writes, "In the end, achievement can't really answer the big questions—Who am I? What am I really worth? How do I face death? It gives the initial illusion of an answer. There is an initial rush of happiness that leads us to believe we have arrived, been included, been accepted, and proved ourselves. However, the satisfaction quickly fades."[10]

As we surveyed similarities and differences in how men and women perceive, define, and pursue satisfaction in their work, we found that both men and women place a high premium on feeling authentic at work.[11] They both agreed with assertions such as, "I seek congruence between my feelings and my actions" and "I strive to be the same person at work and at home." Yet, achieving this kind of alignment can be difficult for women because what they notice, value, and believe the world should be often runs counter to the culture they find at work. In order to make their best contribution, women must find a way to communicate and build support for what they most authentically see.

CHAPTER TWO

Why What Women See Matters

When women speak the truth about what they see, women, organizations, and the world reap the rewards. Women gain energy and a sense of purpose by connecting what is best in themselves with what they seek to accomplish. Organizations access fresh ideas and perspectives by learning to value intuitive insight along with analytical skills. And the world moves toward a safer and more sustainable understanding of what constitutes progress by framing it in a broader social context.

What women see, therefore, *matters.*

It matters especially given the interconnected nature of today's global environment, in which mistakes have consequences that can reverberate unexpectedly in far corners of the world. We can no longer afford—as individuals or as citizens of the planet—to operate from an artificially restricted pool of data that ignores the diverse richness of what human beings perceive; the cost of doing so has simply become too high. Addressing the complexities of our common future requires us to see the world from a full perspective, employing a wide lens as well as a sharp focus.

Doing so requires incorporating what women see at the strategic level, which is why leveraging the female vision is ultimately a *leadership* issue. Although the last thirty years have witnessed a steady influx of women into many sectors—finance, media, government, medicine, law, the military, higher education, and religion—women continue to lack influence when it comes to shaping the big picture. They participate in figuring out the *hows* and the *whats*—the tactics, the implementation—but are less often in the position to decide the *whys* and the *ifs*. Women have gained a seat at the table, but since what they see is rarely included in the big conversations that determine the overarching purpose, their most authentic and distinctive gifts often remain locked within them.

Most organizations understand that the development of women leaders is desirable. And they know they must get better at attracting and retaining talented women. They recognize—as Catalyst founder Felice Schwartz argued nearly two decades ago—that women constitute a business imperative.[1] But they rarely consider that women might also constitute a strategic imperative or provide a source of vision as well as a source of talent.

When this goes unrecognized, the most well-intentioned efforts to recruit, retain, and develop women flounder. Sally saw this when she was working for one of the world's leading technology developers—which we'll call "Macro Solutions." The company had expended significant resources trying to bring more women into leadership positions. It set targets for hiring women engineers and partnered with engineering schools to develop a stronger pipeline of skilled women. It implemented a cascade of programs—flextime, work-from-home options, onsite care for sick children—aimed at securing a place on lists of "the best places for women to work." It hired diversity consultants to create a state-of-the-art women's initiative and build a range of affinity networks. And it sent its most senior executives to women's leadership events to demonstrate the company's support.

It worked, but it didn't work well.

Although female attrition slowed, Macro Solutions still had trouble attracting and retaining talented women. The company offered premium salaries, so it had little trouble meeting recruitment targets; however, the most highly sought female candidates often decided to go elsewhere once they saw how few women made it to the leadership level. Women also continued to leave the company at a higher rate then men, and did so at an earlier point in their careers. A number of very visible high potentials either stalled out or took themselves off the leadership track by choosing individual contributor status, further diminishing the pool from which senior women would be drawn.

Despite the company's efforts, internal surveys showed that women still perceived Macro Solutions to be dominated by an old boys network; except for the perks, they did not view it as a great place to work. Women also found the pace to be unsustainable, believed the company wasted time and resources pursuing objectives that didn't contribute to long-term value, and perceived that connections rather than merit influenced promotions. Women rated the company particularly low when asked to score this question: "Do you think your leadership team values women's ideas?"

What had gone wrong?

One day, Sally asked a member of the executive team what the women's leadership initiative was intended to accomplish. He said its purpose was to "bring in and promote more women and make sure they stayed with the company."

But how did he believe this would *help* the company? Why was it important? How would having more women improve the organization's long-term market position or enable it to reach its larger goals?

"We don't see it in those terms," said the executive. "This is a *talent* issue. Plus, we think it's the right thing to do."

In other words, Macro Solutions viewed its women's initiative as a stand-alone effort, the value of which was both self-evident and strictly limited. The company simply wanted to become better at attracting and retaining women: that was the goal. This is fine as far as it goes, but by failing to embed this goal in a larger strategic frame, the company signaled that it wanted to keep on operating as it always had. It wanted more women in high positions, more female faces at the table, but it did not want those women to change the *what* or the *why* of how the business was done. Macro Solutions was eager to enlist women's talents, but it had no desire to leverage the power of women's vision.

Compartmentalizing talent and vision in this way is a manifestation of the one-sided, silo'd approach to enterprise that typified the industrial era. In a knowledge-based economy (and Macro Solutions is nothing if not a knowledge-based business), an organization's value is vested in its people's skill and capacity for innovation, which means that talent and strategy are inextricably linked. By choosing to view women's leadership as a *women's* issue rather than a leadership concern, Macro

Solutions ignored this link. In doing so, it deprived itself of a vital resource for pursuing the kind of systemic change it would need to stay ahead of the curve in a more diverse and integrated marketplace.

Talent initiatives deprived of strategic context are always vulnerable to the ups and downs of the business cycle. They are among the first programs to be cut when times get tough because they are not viewed as essential to the organization's larger mission nor vital to its bedrock values. By compartmentalizing talent from strategy, companies like Macro Solutions send an unwitting message that their women's initiatives are a cyclical rather than a fundamental concern. This reinforces the belief among those resistant to change that the company's focus on women is just another short-term fad.

When Women Leave

The dilemma faced by Macro Solutions typifies a problem that has been developing since the mid-1990s. Women have continued to enter the workplace in growing numbers; in some sectors, they now comprise over 50 percent of the workforce.[2] Yet companies still struggle to hold onto the best female talent.

The "female brain drain," as it is popularly known, presents particular problems at senior and leadership levels.[3] When women fill the ranks but don't make it to the top, those who hold less senior positions are likely to become discouraged about their prospects within the company. A paucity of senior women also strengthens the impression that the organization is run by an old boys network. This in turn creates negative perceptions among female clients and customers, who increasingly prefer to do business with companies they view as women-friendly. For all these reasons, companies that lose top women tend to get caught in a self-reinforcing cycle: women leave, which makes more women consider leaving.

It wasn't supposed to be this way. Up until the mid-1990s, expectations for women as leaders were very high. Women flooded business and professional schools and began surpassing men in educational achievement in almost every field except engineering. Women also began starting their own businesses at a higher rate than men. These demographic trends put pressure on organizations to invest resources in developing and promoting women, and many made a commitment to do so. The effort received an impetus when several influential studies documented a correlation between the number of women in senior positions and superior overall performance.[4]

Yet even as the case for developing women leaders grew stronger, women's *progress* as leaders slowed. Researchers proposed various theories to explain this trend. Perhaps the problem was the lack of female mentors or the persistence of rigid career paths that didn't take women's multiple responsibilities into account. Maybe not enough women chose to work in operations or in line positions rather than staff jobs such as human resources or communications. Maybe women were too reluctant to accept global assignments. Maybe women should start playing golf. Or maybe women had gotten into the pipeline too late; now that more women were filling the pipeline, the problem would end up solving itself.

Partnership firms were particularly active in the effort to develop and retain talented women. This is not surprising. The value of professional services firms is vested entirely in their people, so they spend heavily on the development of potential partners. Losing skilled employees at the associate level, just below partnership, is costly both because it represents a loss of money invested in training and because partners depend on the work of associates to meet client demands. Yet it has been at the associate level that women are most likely to leave. Even firms that try to hire 50 percent women often have a pool of 20 percent by the time these hires reach partnership level.

Several world-class comprehensive efforts aimed at improving these figures produced results. For example, the accounting firm Deloitte was able to triple the number of female partners in the course of a decade.[5] Ernst & Young doubled the number of female partners during the same period of time.[6] Yet progress for senior women in most organizations has remained slow. By the late 1990s, the number of women in senior or board positions in the Fortune 500 had leveled out at around 15 percent, where it has remained stuck ever since.[7] Even the most optimistic observers began to realize that the growing number of women in the workforce was not about to translate into increased influence and power anytime soon.

The stall in women's progress has been surprising because the shift to a knowledge-based economy seemed to support women's talents, skills, and capabilities. The need for companies to connect directly with customers and clients *should have* supported women's skill at building relationships. The trend toward more weblike organizations *should have* supported women's comfort with leading from the center rather than the top. The spread of technologies that facilitated, even demanded, direct communication *should have* supported the female propensity to keep in touch and work well in collaborative settings. Women's vaunted intuition *should have* been a plus in organizations that were traversing uncharted waters and becoming increasingly reliant on innovation. Greater diversity in the workforce *should have* speeded women's rise.

Yet, although these trends did give women an edge, other aspects of the new environment worked against them. For one thing, it was ironic that women had come into the workforce in significant numbers at *precisely the same time* that work was becoming more demanding and more intense. As the global economy ramped up during the long boom of the 1990s and the amount of capital available for mergers and acquisitions soared, organizations came under constant pressure to do more with less, and required people to work harder and longer hours. The successive economic slowdowns of the first decade in the new century only added to the pressure.

Evolving technologies also provided the means for people to work anytime anywhere, creating 24/7 expectations while eroding industrial-era protective barriers between work and home. For example, until the start of the 1990s, most good jobs required around fifty hours a week, constant business travel was uncommon except for those in sales, and no one was expected to field calls during a child's soccer game. As work became more invasive, many of those who had a choice began to rethink their ambitions.

The Opt-Out Fallacy

The popular media has traditionally depicted women who leave their organizations or decline leadership roles as motivated by the simple desire to stay at home. A hotly debated

2006 *New York Times Magazine* cover story proclaiming the advent of the "Opt-Out Revolution" described Ivy League women who preferred playing tennis and scheduling children's playdates to slogging it out in the business world.[8] *Fortune* magazine has a long history of profiling female executives said to have "quit the rat race," abandoning promising careers to devote their energies to the full-time care of their families.[9] Television talk shows routinely pit conservative pundits who cite the exodus of women from top positions as proof that they should have stayed home with their kids in the first place against those who deny that women are discouraged or who content themselves with denouncing male power structures.

But demographic studies tell a more nuanced story. To begin with, women who step aside from demanding business careers rarely leave the workforce altogether. Rather than dropping out, those with education and skills usually choose to pursue a different kind of work, work for a different kind of company, or start a business of their own.

As a result, female work patterns tend to unfold as spirals rather than proceeding along straight lines. The popular media image of "stay-at-home moms" inhabiting a different universe and having different concerns than single-track career women therefore misrepresents a complex and shifting reality. Even women who *do* stay home when their children are young usually return to full-time work within several years.

For example, Myra Hart of the Harvard Business School documented a strong trend among female MBAs exiting corporations and partnership firms in order to work in the social or nonprofit sector.[10] These women often took significant pay cuts in the process. The women in Hart's study reported being motivated by the desire to make a more meaningful contribution to the world and the belief that alternative kinds of work would enable them to live more balanced lives.

Similarly, Wanda Wallace, a researcher at the University of North Carolina, surveyed senior executive women who had either left or were considering leaving their companies.[11] She found that these women were primarily motivated by dissatisfaction with the direction of their organization, a negative change in organizational climate or culture, the belief that their contributions were not valued, the desire to do something worthwhile for society, or feelings of being isolated and disconnected at work.

The women in Wallace's study mentioned family conflict *only as a secondary factor* in their decision to leave their jobs. Family concerns thus provided an additional rationale only if women were otherwise unhappy, but these concerns alone were not sufficient cause for women to leave jobs that they enjoyed or really believed were important.[12] Wallace's survey subjects, like those of Myra Hart, wanted above all to feel that their work mattered to the world.

Women's career decisions are more likely to be motivated by what psychologist Steven Pinker calls "intrinsic rewards"— those they find personally meaningful—than by money or status.[13] Family concerns may play a part in their decisions to stay with or leave a job because family is part of how women perceive intrinsic rewards. But the primary driver for women is the desire to do work that they feel *matters*. Our own research on differences in how men and women perceive, define, and pursue satisfaction at work, presented in chapter 5, supports and reinforces this view.[14]

This preference for intrinsic rewards lies at the heart of the conundrum about why talented women leave. The problem can't be fixed tactically—by offering mentoring programs or flextime, for example—although such accommodations are important. The question of purpose, of what an organization is trying to achieve in the world, must also be addressed. This requires integrating what women see and value into how the organization conceives its role in the world.

Hope Greenfield, former head of talent management at Lehman Brothers, was once asked if so few women held high positions in her company because of a pipeline problem. She said this was the case, but noted it was important to look at the underlying reason. "There's no pipeline," she said, "for the simple reason that women who are now in their forties looked around and said, '*I don't want that.*'" In other words, women did not necessarily perceive the often substantial rewards offered by Lehman Brothers as sufficient motivation for staying with the company throughout their careers.

In the end, this focus on what matters is what makes the female vision so important. As we'll see in the following chapter, many companies in the last decade got caught in the trap of defining value and purpose in ever more narrow terms. This proved to be bad for people, bad for organizations, and bad for the world. To reverse the trend, what women see needs to be incorporated at the strategic level.

CHAPTER THREE

Early Warning Signals

The limitations of one-sided vision were on vivid display in the financial problems that engulfed the world throughout 2008. Although the crisis reflected structural, economic, and political problems that had been brewing for over a decade, it also constituted a *leadership* crisis of epic proportions—a crisis that remains in the aftermath of the meltdown.

This is ironic given that many of the high flyers whose actions led to the threatened financial collapse came from companies that prided themselves on having strong leadership cultures. These companies boasted of hiring the best talent on earth, poured resources into grooming employees deemed to have high potential, and showered their stars with extravagant rewards aimed at driving superior performance and affirming their status as the best and the brightest.

How then did poor decision making, negligible oversight, and disastrously short-term focus become endemic in these very organizations? Where did the best and the brightest go awry? How did an apparently rational system based on quantitative analysis and justified by predictive modeling manage to get the basic numbers wrong? And why did companies fail to recognize that offering $10-million bonuses might actually serve as a mechanism for attracting and motivating the most avaricious and ego-driven?

Given its scope, the financial crisis that erupted in 2008 was not simply a story of bad apples. Nor was it just a cautionary tale about human greed. It was rather a demonstration of what can happen when an exceedingly narrow vision gains ascendancy in the business culture and continues to operate without check. In many of the organizations implicated in the meltdown, a single-minded focus on maximizing short-term profit—piously justified as "creating shareholder value"— overwhelmed other concerns, such as building capacity for the future, serving customers and clients, and providing resources for new industries and enterprises.

In our profoundly interconnected global economy, this narrow vision exposed a broad swath of businesses to enormous risk, raising plenty of alarms in advance. But even obvious dangers were dismissed by a blinkered leadership culture focused on making the next quarter's numbers. It was precisely this culture that talented women—women who had accumulated the right degrees and experience, women who seemed to be on a trajectory to the top—were, by the mid-1990s, beginning to reject.

They were women like those Myra Hart had studied, who earned MBAs at elite Ivy League schools, joined prestigious firms, and then shifted course to work for nonprofits because they didn't see a fit between their values and those of the companies they had joined.[1] They were women like Wanda Wallace had interviewed, who felt disconnected from their companies and yearned to do something more worthwhile with their lives.[2] They were, quite simply, the women who had left.

Where Were the Women?

In part because of attrition and derailment and in part because of the persistence of the glass ceiling, women were underrepresented in senior positions in the companies implicated in the financial crisis—on Wall Street, but also in London, Sydney, Reykjavik, Dublin, Geneva, and Dubai. And women were almost entirely missing from the ranks of high-stakes dealmakers, merger-and-acquisition kings, buyout artists, and hedge fund entrepreneurs, whose access to capital had transformed the nature of finance in the decade before the meltdown.

Although women comprised the majority in many sectors of the workforce and had become proportionately better educated and more professionally skilled than men in many fields, they were not for the most part making the big financial decisions or placing the big bets. They were not pushing through the deals that changed how things were done. In the big leagues of finance, women still played mostly second string.

The absence of senior women in the companies implicated in the meltdown did not go unnoticed. As the financial journalist Michael Lewis observed in 2008, "One of the distinctive traits of the financial disaster was . . . how little women had to do with it."[3] The *Financial Times* pondered whether more input from women board members or executives might have put a brake on the kind of overleveraged gambles that had led to the disaster, and noted that Iceland had recently turned to two female bankers to save its bankrupt system from complete collapse.[4] *New York Times* columnist Nicholas Kristof referenced a Cambridge University study linking high testosterone levels to risky behavior and wondered if male hormones might have precipitated the crisis.[5] The *Washington Post*, in an article datelined London, noted that "Fred, Tom, Andy, Dennis, Eric, John, Stephen, Antonio and Paul ran British banks that lost billions of dollars," and quoted Sir Howard Archer, chief European and UK economist at IHS Global Insight in London, as saying, "You can argue that the men have made a right mess of it, and now the ladies should have a go."[6]

The author Jason Zweig, the *Wall Street Journal*'s personal finance columnist, made the case baldly in *The Little Book of Safe Money*, noting "The masters of the universe turned out to be masters of disaster. No matter which aspect of the financial crisis you consider—there is a man behind it." Zweig attributed this to the emotional differences in how men and women perceive and take risks. He quoted Vickie Bajtelsmit, chair of the finance department at Colorado State: "Women care less than men about the adrenaline rush, the play element and the bragging rights that come from trading competitively."[7]

Many women had no problem seeing the connection Zweig would later make between the meltdown and the dominant leadership culture they had watched emerge since the mid-1990s. Julie heard about it from her highly accomplished female clients, some of whom had been passed over for top jobs in financial services, some who had left their companies, some who had stayed where they were and made their peace even though they retained doubts about the direction their organizations were going. Many of these women had come of age in companies that emphasized building long-term value, only to see this commitment abandoned in the race to embrace ever more aggressive growth.

Watching the crisis unfold dismayed these women but also gave many of them a new confidence in the value of their own perceptions. "I guess I *did* know what I was talking about," said one, summing up a consensus view. "I guess my concerns about where we were heading *were* justified. Every time I raised a red flag, my male colleagues threw a bunch of numbers on the board to show why everything would be fine. I was viewed as too cautious, and I came to doubt myself. But I'm not going to be so quick to doubt what I see in the future."

Sally heard a similar drumbeat of female skepticism in October 2008, when she spoke at the Women's Forum for the Economy and Society in Deauville, France. The participants, a normally decorous contingent of senior women from around the world, were riled up and eager to talk about how some of the most lionized male leaders on earth had led their companies, their countries, and their economies toward disaster. In panels, roundtables, at lunches, and in question-and-answer sessions, participants took to the microphones to declare that they would no longer back off from articulating what they knew and saw.

"They told us we had to wait," one woman proclaimed during an after-luncheon forum. "They told us we didn't know enough, didn't have the right credentials. They told us we weren't ready to serve on the important boards because we hadn't managed $50-million lines of business. But some of the most qualified men in the world got us into this world-historic mess. Women can't afford to buy into the myth of our own inadequacy anymore!"

Of course, we will never know if having more women on boards or positions of power could have averted or softened the crisis. But it's clear in retrospect that an unbalanced leadership culture led some famed institutions over the cliff. Jacki Zehner, a former partner at Goldman Sachs, responded by funding a study with the National Council for Research on Women. The study finds that female hedge fund mangers are less willing to assume a high degree of risk, less likely to take an attitude of "no guts, no glory."[8] As Zehner observes, "The companies [implicated in the crisis] needed more women leaders because they needed a more balanced decision-making model. Think what might have happened if Lehman Brothers had been Lehman Brothers and Sisters!"

The big problem was that the dominant culture—the culture in which Lehman Sisters were absent—offered women few opportunities to act upon what they noticed. But that didn't stop women from noticing what was going on. They *noticed* that Vegas-style betting and a winner-take-all management style were hollowing out long-term value. They *noticed* that downsizing aimed at wowing the markets was often used to justify bloated pay-for-performance executive contracts. They *noticed* that corporate boards with 85 percent male leadership (the average) often did a remarkably poor job of reining in executives addicted to risk who rewarded themselves handsomely even when things were going wrong. They *noticed* that turbo-charged growth strategies and relentless acquisitions were often the result of numbers games that looked good on paper but did nothing to improve products, services, or customer satisfaction. And they *noticed* that their own progress seemed to have stalled while executives with dubious track records—some of whom had been leaving trails of wreckage behind them for decades—seemed to land on their feet.

Above all, women noticed that the quality of their own lives and the lives of those around them was deteriorating as organizations absorbed more risk and put more pressure on their people. It wasn't just that people were working too hard and too long—although they often were. The larger problem lay with a system that had assumed a momentum of its own— a momentum that was out of sync with what most human beings require in order to live satisfying and harmonious lives.

Extreme demands were creating an extreme workplace, giving the most unbalanced and financially driven individuals an edge. These individuals in turn set the tone by hiring and promoting others who shared their values and their single-minded commitment to financial reward. Pay-for-performance contracts ratcheted up the intensity, with performance interpreted as the willingness to devote every waking hour to work. Talented people who valued balance, family life, or simply having sufficient time to make thoughtful decisions were seen as insufficiently tough or deemed to be underachievers. Not surprisingly, many women failed to thrive in this environment.

So the question posed by the *Financial Times* about whether more women in positions of power could have prevented the risky and grandiose wagers that led to disaster *gets things precisely backward*. Rather, the underrepresentation of women in senior positions was both a consequence and a symptom of a leadership culture that had grown increasingly unbalanced.

The inability of women to feel deeply engaged by this culture should have provided an early warning signal that trouble was brewing. But companies chose to view the retention of senior women as a *women's* issue rather than a strategic or leadership concern. They compartmentalized the problem and so failed to see the link between talented women dropping by the wayside and a business culture focused on short-term and at times dubiously defined "results" to the exclusion of everything else. Both the goals and the methods of this culture were unsustainable. Companies were burning through profits as they burned through people.

Fail-Safe

Before the crisis erupted, some very high-profile senior women stepped forward to warn that short-term profits in the financial sector were masking long-term problems. For example, the financial analyst Meredith Whitney shocked the markets by forecasting in 2007 that Citigroup would have to drop its dividend because of a leaky balance sheet.[9] Whitney predicted losses and write-downs for Lehman Brothers, Bank of America, and Merrill Lynch at a time when these companies were viewed as rock solid in the marketplace. She also criticized the ratings agencies for their incestuous relationships with the big banks and questioned the accuracy and, in some cases, the honesty of the ratings agencies' numbers.[10]

Sheila Bair, chair of the Federal Deposit Insurance Corporation (FDIC), was also busy raising the alarm about the dangers of subprime lending.[11] When the government was finally forced to deal with the issue, Bair very publicly objected that the terms of the bank bailout did not protect mortgage holders, a weakness she believed would undermine its effectiveness in the years ahead.[12] Her objections infuriated Treasury Department officials, who mocked her as an overcautious scold, incapable of understanding the numbers.

Brooksley Born, former chair of the Commodity Futures Trading Commission, spent much of the decade before the meltdown trying to raise concerns about unregulated derivative contracts. She believed that the growing popularity of instruments such as credit default swaps and their extension to high-risk mortgages was exposing the entire economy to risk.[13] Born's principal antagonist in Washington DC had been Federal Reserve chair Alan Greenspan, who dismissed her as a plodding bureaucrat, hostile to entrepreneurial effort and too stuck in the past to appreciate the potential benefits of financial innovation.[14]

In 2009, Bair and Born received the JFK Profile in Courage award for their efforts to raise awareness of the impending crisis.[15] At the ceremony, Bair said she was "particularly pleased to be joining other female awardees who stood up when their male counterparts failed to act, or worse, actively fought them."[16] The mainstream business press, reporting Bair's remarks and noting that a disproportionate number of astute warnings had come from women, described the fact that the awardees were women as a simple coincidence.

This brought a sense of what Yogi Berra famously described as "déjà vu all over again." It provided an almost exact reprise of the experience of January 2003, when *Time* magazine designated three women as its "Persons of the Year."[17] Sherron Watkins of Enron, Cynthia Cooper of WorldCom, and Colleen Rowley at the FBI had all tried to draw the attention of their superiors to practices that they believed were leading their organizations toward disaster. In paying tribute to the foresight and courage exercised by these women, *Time* optimistically declared that recognizing their accomplishments would constitute a "fail-safe system" that would keep organizations from following ruinous practices in the years ahead. The editors also opined that the women had "kick-started a conversation essential to the clean operation of American life, a conversation that will continue for years."[18]

That conversation, of course, fizzled out, and the fail-safe system failed to keep anyone safe, not just in the United States but around the world. Within a year, self-aggrandizing and shortsighted leaders at companies far more consequential than WorldCom or Enron were once again exposing the public to extraordinary risk.

Time's editors asked rhetorically if gender had anything to do with the women's actions and concluded that it did not. But Sherron Watkins later observed that being a woman, in fact, had a lot to do with the actions she had taken at Enron. Keynoting the annual Simmons College Women's Leadership Conference in Boston in the spring of 2003, Watkins described her efforts to draw Enron CEO Ken Lay's attention to the accounting practices that would in short order lead to the company's demise.[19]

She noted that, as a woman, she was always an outsider in Enron's vociferously male culture, a circumstance she believed gave her a broader perspective about what was going on. She noted that many of the men she worked with positively thrived on risk, boasting about throwing "Hail Mary passes" and wagering huge amounts on bets that were at best uncertain. She was also skeptical about the numbers games the men around her seemed to be engaged in playing, the unorthodox accounting schemes that made no sense but looked good on paper. The "special purpose entities" with names like Raptor and Condor struck her as childish, representative of an attitude that saw business and risk as nothing more than a game.

Watkins also said that the unremitting, punishing pace of her work made it easier for her to take the bold (if ultimately futile) step of trying to warn her boss of potential problems, because it caused her to put her job within a broader perspective. She noted that many of the men in the company had abdicated family concerns to their wives; for them, working 24/7 was a badge of honor rather than a source of potential conflict. Watkins believed that having primary responsibility for her small daughter grounded her and kept her focused on what really mattered in life. Enron provided her with a livelihood, but not an identity. She felt loyal to the company, but she could imagine life without it.

In her session at Simmons, Watkins connected the dots between the "no guts, no glory" culture typified by turn-of-this-century Enron and the practices that were driving talented women out of high-profile positions. Drawing from her own experience, she made clear why women in high positions often felt ambivalent about jobs they had worked very hard to attain. She demonstrated why being an outsider made her more disposed to question company practices in a way that someone fully *of* the culture would not. And she clarified how having multiple responsibilities at work and at home gave her a broader and longer-term perspective than male colleagues who focused all their attention on their work.

Enron was an energy company that morphed into a financial trading enterprise whose supposed expertise lay in the development of complex trading models. This history gives it special resonance as a cautionary tale. The energy sector began as a classic industrial-era business whose purpose was to exploit and transport natural resources. For the most part, such companies have honored the frontier imperative that shaped how the west was won: *get while the gettin's good and get out!*

Enron adapted this frontier approach to fit the world of finance and trading, racking up spectacular profits in order to *get while the gettin' was good*. True to its original model, it left the earth scorched in its wake. But although the company crashed and burned, the cultural attitude it pioneered went on to flourish, and the leadership style it exalted gained a foothold in many of the banks and insurance companies that would later be brought low by the financial meltdown.

Traders at Enron used complex mathematical formulas to justify wildly overleveraged bets. The impenetrability of these abstract formulas made transparency difficult and enabled the company to conceal losses that had been taking place for years. The complexity forestalled questions from outsiders by tossing up a blizzard of equations—if you weren't smart enough to understand them, the thinking went, you probably shouldn't be asking questions. The true purpose, as it turned out, was to keep everything going just a little longer, extracting maximum profits until the end. That's the essence of the frontier model—the end of the getting is always *gettin' out*, the expression of a purposefully short-term and narrow vision.

Vision and the Seer

Women like Sheila Bair and Brooksley Born, as well as *Time*'s 2003 "Persons of the Year," tried to exert leadership in a manner that was consistent with what they saw, what they valued, and what they believed the world should be. But their ideas failed to gain acceptance at the decision-making level until after what they had warned against had come to pass.

These women thus found themselves playing the time-honored role of Cassandra prophesying disasters that they were powerless to avert. It is no coincidence that Cassandra, the mythic embodiment of fruitless early warning, is a woman. In the Greek legend, Cassandra was the daughter of Priam, king of Troy. When the god Apollo fell in love with her, he gave her the gift of prophecy, which he could bestow but was powerless to revoke. When Cassandra failed to return Apollo's love, the only way he could punish her was by decreeing that nobody would believe anything she said. So, although Cassandra foresaw the destruction of Troy, she could not save her homeland from tragedy because her warnings were doomed to be ignored.

Cassandra has been known as the "cursed prophetess." Her fate demonstrates what happens when women's vision has no power, and her myth set the stage for three thousand years of women's insights being dismissed. Yet Cassandra's gifts—her outsider eyes, her sense of perspective, her ability to notice and connect the dots—have survived in the concept of "female intuition." Intuition is defined as the ability to acquire knowledge without the use of deductive or inductive analysis; it comes from the Latin *intueri*, which translates as "to look inside."

Intuition offers insights that resist being quantified or measured. As a form of intelligence, it is perceptual and governed by subjective logic. The "right brain" is popularly associated with intuitive processes, such as aesthetic perception and innovation, while the left brain is associated with logic and numbers. Although Western culture has famously privileged logic, more subjective ways of observing, perceiving, and defining value offer a powerful and often profoundly accurate means of knowing. Women's long history of looking inward and trusting intuitive leaps can be a gift to organizations that need to broaden the scope of their information about the world. And as our tales of modern-day Cassandras show, this information is often essential.

PART II

*Elements of
the Female Vision*

CHAPTER FOUR

Broad-Spectrum Notice

The first component that shapes our vision is our capacity to notice. What we notice determines what we see. What we notice also informs how we understand events, order information, and assign value. Our individual style of noticing is an expression of our character, our talents, and our interests. What we notice makes us who we are.

Men and women often have different styles of noticing—not always, but often enough to make a meaningful distinction. As noted in chapter 1, researchers find that men tend to focus deeply and narrowly on a single perception or task, whereas women's attention is often simultaneously engaged by many different things.[1] In one of his last stories, Saul Bellow memorably described one of his characters as a "first-class noticer."[2] Women are often first-class noticers, accustomed to gleaning information from a wide range and variety of sources.

This is hardly surprising. Women's domestic experience, socialization, and evolutionary development have accustomed them to monitoring emotional cues, anticipating what others might need, and making subtle adjustments in order to avoid potential conflicts. Researchers find that women tend to be more skilled than men at reading other people's moods; they pay closer attention to tone of voice and facial expression, and draw more accurate conclusions about how others are responding.[3] Their observations color their perception of events, adding a subjective element to how they understand situations.

The author Jason Zweig, quoted previously, believes that women's antennae and sensitivity to nonverbal gestures and expressions can make them better at gauging whether someone is trustworthy or not. He notes that "women may be more likely to spot tell-tale signs of dishonesty if they step into a conversation that is already underway. A man may already be caught up in a bond of developing trust whereas a woman will bring a more objective outsider perspective."[4]

These two types of notice complement one another. Broad-spectrum notice is good at judging context and making unexpected connections, while focused notice provides clarity and analytic rigor. Broad-spectrum notice resists quantification and can seem overly subjective, but focused notice can leave out vital information. Women and men flourish when they both feel comfortable sharing the richness of what they notice, and organizations can benefit as a result.

In this book's opening anecdote, we saw what happens when broad-spectrum notice is ignored. Jill *noticed* the general tenor of the meeting and watched how people in the room reacted, while Jim focused on the sales manager who was making the presentation. Jill did not ignore the presentation; she simply noticed other things that were going on and set the scene within a larger frame. For Jim, the presentation *was* the frame, the single point of reference.

Jill immediately backed down when Jim challenged the relevance of her observations. This often happens in workplace situations. Because broad-spectrum notice has not traditionally been recognized as having value in organizations, women often hesitate to assert and defend the value of what they see. They may feel they don't have the language to do so, or they may doubt the validity of their observations. But by *not* making their case for what they notice, women diminish their own capacity for authentic contribution and undermine their real power at work.

Susan Bernstein, now an independent coach and consultant, provides a perfect example of what can happen when the value of broad-spectrum notice is overlooked. [5] Fresh out of an MBA program, she went to work for a large consulting firm, which assigned her to work with a major apparel manufacturer. A few days after she took the job, her manager asked her to attend a meeting of the client's senior leaders, saying, "Your job is just to notice what's going on."

"*What* do you want me to notice?" Susan asked.

"Whatever seems important. And don't forget to keep good notes."

At the meeting, Susan was immediately struck by the hostility between the two senior executives who ran the division. It was evident in the way Dave rolled his eyes when Bob was speaking, and in Bob's refusal to acknowledge Dave's remarks.

After the meeting, Susan's boss asked what she had noticed. She said, "I noticed that Dave and Bob don't seem to like one another."

"How could you possibly know that?" her boss demanded.

Susan consulted her notes and started to share specific observations. Her manager cut her off. "That's not what you were there for."

"I thought I was just supposed to notice."

"I was referring to noticing the business data."

"How can the project be successful if the guys running it are at each others' throats?"

"You are a strategy consultant," Susan's boss instructed. "Judging personalities is the OD [organizational development] consultant's job. If you're going to succeed at strategy, you need to be completely objective."

Susan took heed and continued with the project, but the pushback she'd received stayed with her for a very long time. She says, "After a couple years on the job, my noticing capacity got stripped out of me. My ability to read verbal cues and discern context just seemed to dry up. I was trying so hard to be objective that I blocked out all kinds of information and purposefully restricted my range of vision. I went native, and lost what was best about myself. It took me years to really get that back."

A female speechwriter at a major corporation found herself in a similar situation, and while the pushback she received was similar, it had a different rationale. Her CEO had asked her to participate in a brainstorming session on how the company could gain greater recognition as a good corporate citizen. The previous evening, the speechwriter had spoken with her sister, a high school teacher, who was lamenting her students' lack of financial literacy. In the morning meeting, the speechwriter cited this conversation and suggested that her company consider partnering with a local school to develop a curriculum on the subject.

"It's a thought," said the CEO, who then tasked the head of corporate communications with putting together a group to look into it.

The speechwriter left the meeting feeling good about her

contribution. But shortly afterward, the head of corporate communications pulled her aside and scolded her for bringing the matter up. In part he was annoyed because she hadn't mentioned the idea to him before the meeting; he was her superior and information was supposed to be channeled through him. But he was primarily upset because he thought her suggestion had been inappropriate.

"Why would the CEO of this company care about your family conversations?" he demanded.

"I just noticed a connection between what my sister saw and what we were trying to do," she said.

"I don't see a link," he said. "And quoting a high school teacher in an executive-level meeting is not exactly impressive. All you did was make yourself look ridiculous."

Her boss's strong reaction caused the speechwriter to question the value of her idea. She went away feeling chastened and the subject was dropped. It was not until six months later, when a competitor launched a financial literacy pilot for high schools that gained national notice, that she recognized her idea had in fact been a good one. Her company could not act upon it, however, because of her boss's insistence on compartmentalizing information; in his view, insights gained from one's personal life had no place in business. The result of this restricted notice was lost opportunity. In retrospect, she wished she had been a stronger advocate for her idea.

Wired to Notice

What accounts for differences in how men and women notice? Why have we evolved in complementary ways? Are divergences only the result of socialization, or of something more fundamental? Recent evidence from the fields of cognitive and social psychology suggests that our different noticing styles may have a biological as well as a cultural basis.

For example, functional MRIs reveal that men (on average) have more "gray matter" in their brains than women, while women have more "white matter" than men.[6] Gray matter consists of neural cells that process information, whereas white matter consists of nerve cell extensions, or axons, that connect these processing centers. Gray matter provides the neural energy required to perform functions that take place in a single area of the brain; white matter distributes and integrates the information in different parts of the brain.[7] With more axons, women's brains have more points of integration and connection, which enables their mental activities to take place in the left and right hemispheres at the same time. This is the primary physiological reason that women are more likely to bring right-brain resources such as intuitive knowing to left-brain situations. For women, logic and intuition are less divided.

Brain imaging also reveals that human beings process information through the cerebral cortex, which is larger in females, has more inputs, and develops at an earlier stage of life.[8] Because this part of the brain regulates memory and emotion, women's perceptions are more likely to be influenced by their feelings. For women, subjectivity is an integral neural aspect of perception. Women's ability to process information is therefore strengthened when their feelings are activated.

Sue Lovell, head of the science department at Miss Hall's School in Pittsfield, Massachusetts, leverages this understanding in her teaching. She says, "I find that if I tell my female students to imagine a ball rolling down a ramp or swinging at the end of a pendulum, many of them will tune out because they have no reason to care. But if I frame the same problem in terms of a dog running down a hill toward traffic, or a child playing on a swing, that gets their attention and engages their problem-solving skills."[9] Lovell points out that girls who have a history of being good at math or science may not need this kind of framing, but others benefit, and their ability to do equations improves.

Of course, biologically based differences are always relative, with individual variations taking place along a spectrum. And since both men and women have the capacity to change even long-established behaviors, viewing gender in too deterministic a frame is inaccurate as well as unfair. New experiences give our brains the resources to build new neural pathways, which means our capacities develop as our circumstances change. Given human adaptability and our ability to make conscious choices—otherwise known as free will—describing any behavior as "innate" can be misleading.

Yet observable biological differences *do* shape how many men and women gather and process information. This in turn influences what we notice. Because most organizations have been developed, led, and staffed by men, it's not surprising that they are structured to support and reward focused notice. Nor is it surprising that organizations find it hard to make use of the perceptual capability that is actually one of women's greatest gifts. The privileging of focused notice handicaps efforts to harness the full potential of what women have to offer. And it can make women lose confidence in the value of what they see.

Yet changes in the larger environment are creating opportunities for organizations to expand the sources of information from which they draw. Focused notice was an asset in the industrial era, when companies sought to offer products and services to the largest possible number of people and operate in the most efficient way. But an overemphasis on focus has become an impediment as markets have grown more fluid and the economy more dependent on human knowledge. Organizations increasingly need to meet highly customized needs that change rapidly and unpredictably over time. Broad-spectrum notice provides an advantage in a marketplace that requires flexibility and punishes rigid beliefs and business models. It opens the doors to new kinds of information and new ways of knowing.

The best organizations have tried to adapt to the new environment by becoming more weblike and inclusive, and adopting a less compartmentalized approach to structure and operations.[10] But companies must also learn to support ways of seeing that accommodate contingency and context, and attend to details that may seem beside the point but are vital for intuiting the future. The complex nature of today's marketplace mirrors the connectivity that white matter provides in the mental sphere. This means companies must get better at supporting broad-spectrum notice.

Notice and Numbers

Focused notice has one clear advantage: its value can often be quantified. Putting numbers around something makes it appear objective. Equations are familiarly known as "proofs," which suggests that numbers do not lie, even though we all know that they sometimes do. Elegant and complex formulas can show profit where none exists, verify impossible results, and prove the mitigation of risk where risk in fact abounds.

Gillian Tett, in *Fool's Gold*, her insightful study of the 2008 financial crisis, notes that many bankers went astray because they viewed their own mathematical models as infallible."[11] She cites as an example how the British holding company HSBC was confounded when a U.S. subsidiary in 2006 reported defaults that defied the bank's economic models. The bankers who were confronting the data had no idea how to account for it because it contradicted the results that their formulas predicted. They had so much faith in their models that when the facts did not fit, they simply decided the facts must be wrong.

Even bankers who didn't use the predominant models assumed that the models were right. Tett describes how Blythe Masters, then CFO of the investment bank at JP Morgan Chase, was confounded in her efforts to figure out how competitors like Goldman Sachs, Merrill Lynch, and Lehman Brothers were managing to reap gigantic profits from collateralized debt without accumulating substantial risk.[12] Masters had been on the team at JP Morgan that pioneered these securities back in the 1990s, and she enjoyed a formidable reputation as a credit innovator. But although JP Morgan had innovated the securitizing of markets through the use of credit derivatives, it refused to apply the same approach to subprime loans because the company's bankers deemed the debt too risky to produce reliable profits.

By 2006, however, the company was being punished in the marketplace for its caution, which is why Masters kept on running the math, trying to figure out how the company's competitors were making it work. Unable to come up with the numbers, she concluded that *she* must be doing something wrong. It never occurred to her that the other banks were accumulating enormous risks by using models that were inaccurate, fallible, and based on false assumptions.

Of course, organizations cannot operate without numbers; balance sheets and profit and loss statements are the lifeblood of every enterprise. But quantitative models have no way to account for the vagaries of human behavior, such as greed, panic, delusion, or the kind of "irrational exuberance" that Federal Reserve chair Alan Greenspan famously denounced but failed to discourage. And formulas by their very nature operate by leaving things out; their very elegance is a product of their limitations.

Even when numbers seem straightforward, they don't tell the whole story. Something is always factored out of the equation. A refrigerator is said to "cost" $450 to manufacture, but this is only because the cost of disposal is assumed by entities other than the buyer. Nations calculate their gross national product (GNP) and report it as fact, but the measures they use leave out such essentials as the productive value of unpaid household labor and childcare, and the cost to productivity of inadequate healthcare. The "P" of GNP is strictly bounded. Decisions about what to include in equations are often arbitrary or reflect a political agenda, as when the United States decided to stop factoring increases in consumer energy costs or college tuition into how it calculated and reported inflation.

The complexity of numbers makes them fungible. They appear solid—as *proofs*—but once they reach a high level of complexity, they can be interpreted to mean different things.

Those who are most skilled at using them understand this. Julie once walked into the office of a senior banker, who was involved in developing the formula for packaging credit derivatives. She was surprised to see an old-fashioned blackboard set up behind him, completely covered with strings of numbers in complex patterns.

"What's that you're working on?" she asked.

He nodded toward the figures.

"That?" he responded. "That's just spaghetti."

The privileging of numbers over other kinds of information can put women at a disadvantage. This is not because they are unskilled with numbers but because women tend to notice what the numbers might leave out; they put the numbers in a larger context. The difficulties posed by nuanced insight can hamper women in business school, where the case study method exalts the role of numerical proofs.

The author Kate Sweetman tells a story that illustrates how this happens.[13] In her first year in a graduate business program, Sweetman took a course in which students were tasked with playing a game that required them to offer products for bid in a series of lightning rounds. Each player's goal was to maximize his or her returns based on differentials between margin and volume. Whoever made the most money at the end of the game would be the winner.

Sweetman was thrilled when the professor calculated the results and announced, "The winner is Mr. Sweetman."

Kate stepped forward to claim her prize. The professor, who seemed flustered because he'd assumed she was a man, shook hands briefly and asked her to describe the algorithm she'd used to calculate her results.

Kate started to explain that she had carefully watched how the bets were placed in each round, then figured her next bid based on the specifics she had observed driving the previous round.

"Just give us your numeric formula," said the professor.

Kate said she hadn't used one. She had simply made a highly informed guess derived from close observation of how the market was reacting. The professor noted that a guess, however accurate or well-informed, did not count in the competition. He turned his back on her and called out the next name on the list. "Would Mr. So-and-so please come to the front of the room? You have won the competition."

Sweetman was embarrassed and confused, figuring she had missed the point of the exercise. She was only in her second month in business school, but she had already in essence been told that her way of reasoning was not legitimate. She swallowed her feelings, internalizing the experience and framing it as basically a failure. Only years later did she recognize that her intuitive response had as much value as answers that had been mathematically derived.

The problem lay not in Kate's inability to devise the right formula, but in her professor's refusal to see beyond the math or acknowledge that diverse methods might yield a correct result. Accuracy was not however what he sought, but rather justification by quantitative measure: a closed system that could be replicated to produce reliable results. The algorithms offered by Sweetman's fellow students did have predictive value, but they were only as powerful as the information programmed into them, and their information had been less robust than hers.

The case study method is by nature highly compartmentalized; it works because it limits the scope of information. It cannot accommodate creativity and intuitive insight, nor can it account for the vagaries of human behavior. Like most closed systems, it spurns the kind of "out-of-the-box" thinking and integrated solutions that organizations these days claim to want and that an uncertain environment rewards. The case-study method gives no quarter to broad-spectrum notice and may be one of the reasons that the number of women entering business schools has begun to decline.

Such unyielding devotion to the quantitative method in business education has recently come under scrutiny. The financial crisis demonstrated the limits of analytic methods and offered a perfect example of what happens when the human context of business is ignored. As a result, rational economic theory, which offers predictive models based on the assumption that people and markets are always efficient calcu-lators of self-interest, has begun losing ground to behavioral economics, which better accommodates context and broad-spectrum notice.

Notice and Relationships

Broad-spectrum noticers are mentally engaged by observing other people. They devote energy to reading mood, feelings, and tone. Attuned to the fine points of interaction, they are often highly skilled at building relationships. And they place high value on their ability to do so.

In researching *The Female Advantage: Women's Ways of Leadership*, Sally found that the best women leaders tend to judge the quality of their organizations based on the quality of relationships within them. They not only value and attend to their own relationships with others but also seek to build organizations in which relationships at every level can thrive.[14] Similarly, Margaret Heffernan, in her excellent study of female entrepreneurs, found that successful women business owners consciously build relationship-centric organizations in order to create loyalty among female employees.[15]

A Roosevelt University team found that "a relationship-oriented climate" was *the number one* factor in determining a woman's commitment to her organization. As the authors noted, "When women perceive a deterioration in the social aspects of the work environment, they consider exiting the organization."[16] Similarly, Israeli researchers found that "there appears to be a greater sensitivity among women to the social milieu of the workplace. As a result, the state of personal relationships is paramount to whether they stay or leave."[17]

Why do women place so much value on relationships? Recent advances in neuroscience suggest some answers. A UCLA lab team using functional MRIs found that humans register the social pain of isolation and rejection in the same areas of the brain and with the same intensity as they register physical pain.[18] Further investigation revealed that women experience social pain more acutely than men and in more parts of the brain simultaneously. Another study using similar methodology revealed that the hippocampus, which constitutes the major memory center in the brain, is more active in women when they are interacting with others. This makes women more likely to remember the details of emotional exchanges and personal conversations.[19]

UCLA social psychologist Shelley Taylor presents evidence

that the popularly described "fight or flight" instinct operates differently in women and men.[20] Instead of responding aggressively or fleeing the scene when danger presents itself, women react by "tending and befriending," broadening and deepening relationships with others in order to mitigate stress. Taylor noted that lab research reveals that tending and befriending behavior in women stimulates the release of oxytocin, a neurohormone that calms the central nervous system and promotes a feeling of connection with others.

Oxytocin operates similarly in men and women. But testosterone, which is stimulated in men by the appearance of danger, blocks its action, whereas estrogen seems to enhance its effects. It's therefore little wonder that relationships are so important to women. Human connection provides the primary physiological resource that enables women to cope with stress.

Organizations that support strong relationships create an oxytocin-rich environment that gives women the resources they need to thrive. As noted in chapter 3, researcher Wanda Wallace found that women experience loneliness and isolation in organizations as intolerable, a sufficient reason for leaving what might otherwise be a good job.[21] Men, who have dealt with loneliness at work for generations, seem to be less likely to consider leaving because they feel disconnected. As executive coach Marshall Goldsmith observes, "In general, men have not expected to get their relationship needs met at work. If they feel isolated, they just suck it up."[22] Women, having a lower tolerance for isolation and experiencing a greater need to tend and befriend, are apt to place a higher value on work that provides satisfying relationships.

The value women place on relationships has increasing marketplace value. Changes in the nature of technology have made relationships—with customers, clients, suppliers, competitors, shareholders, and the community as well as within the organization itself—a far more vital resource for organizations than in years past. Twenty years ago, relationships were considered the soft stuff, dismissed as the province of "human resource weenies" by those who valued strategic toughness. Today, they are more likely to be seen as essential to innovation, teamwork, customer satisfaction, talent retention, and the transmission of embodied wisdom.

In *A Whole New Mind,* author Daniel Pink describes why the changing nature of work has made relationships more important.[23] He notes that the industrial and information ages valued analytic skills and the ability to follow the kind of predefined rules that are enshrined in procedural manuals or software code. Attention to these rules enabled people in organizations to wring value from the production of replicable products.

Pink shows how our present "conceptual age" locates value in creativity, which is enhanced when empathy and collaboration are present. He therefore predicts that an ability to read and interpret "the subtleties of human interaction" will emerge as *the* key leadership competency in the years ahead. Recognizing this should give women greater confidence in the value of their capacity for broad-spectrum notice. This fundamental component of the female vision should serve them well in the years ahead.

CHAPTER FIVE

Satisfaction Day by Day

Just as men and women often have different styles of noticing, so also do men and women often perceive value in different ways. The particular way women perceive value constitutes the second element of the female vision. Women's perception of value gives context to the details they notice. It shapes their judgments about where to invest time, energy, and talents. It determines where they put their attention.

In researching this book, we became aware of differences in how men and women perceive value as we interviewed women who had either left high positions or were considering doing so. Some of these women were clients, others were fellow speakers or panelists at corporate and university events, still others were well-known executives whose decisions were chronicled in the business press. As we listened to their stories, we were struck by a recurring theme, a phrase that we heard time and again.

When asked what specifically had brought them to their decision, the majority summed it up by saying, "I decided it just wasn't worth it."

What does this mean?

It means that the women we spoke with did not perceive the tradeoffs their companies were asking them to make—in terms of time, stress, lifestyle, relationships—to be adequately compensated by the rewards offered in return. It does *not* mean that the women were unwilling to sacrifice their time or to live with the adrenaline rush we all experience when we're over-extended or thrillingly involved in our work. It *does* mean that these women did not find their company's traditional reward system sufficiently compelling.

Why not? Why would jobs that have been valued without question by generations of men not necessarily be regarded in the same way by women? Might women perceive worth in a different way? And if so, how might women's perceptions of worth, their vision of what constitutes value, differ from what their companies assume they hold in high regard? And what could be the source of this underlying disjunction?

Over the last two decades, there has been increasing recognition that the *structure* of work was designed to reflect the realities of an all-male workforce whose constituents had few, if any, domestic responsibilities beyond supporting their families. But there has been little thought given to whether the *rewards* of work might also reflect male priorities. Our research suggests a fundamental mismatch between what the marketplace assumes people will value in their work and what women (not all women, but enough to make a difference) most deeply value. This occurs because organizations still offer reward, recognize achievement, build incentive, and decide promotion using definitions of worth that reflect an all-male industrial leadership culture.

Worth and Satisfaction

Hearing women describe prestigious and well-paid jobs as "not worth it" made us realize that we needed a clearer understanding of exactly what this might mean. We had anecdotal examples, but we also needed data. To supply it, we created a survey designed to identify differences and similarities in how men and women perceive, define, and pursue satisfaction in their work.[1]

We believed that focusing on satisfaction rather than seeking to map the more abstract terrain of values would give us a clearer picture of what men and women held to be of value. Because satisfaction is experienced viscerally and because people value that which they perceive as satisfying, focusing on satisfaction gave us a way to explore perceptions of worth.

Our survey was delivered online by Harris Interactive, a division of Harris Polling, to a pool of 818 men and women at companies with a minimum of fifty employees. All held mid-level or higher management positions or were individual contributors with professional skills. Fifty-four percent of respondents were men. Both men and women were drawn from a broad spectrum of industries and sectors. The assessment asked respondents to rate eighty-four items on a scale of 1 to 5, from "does not describe me" to "describes me very well."

We found significant differences in how men and women perceive satisfaction and assign value in their work.[2] For example, the men in our study placed a higher value than the women did on compensation and benefits, which they viewed as intrinsically satisfying, a clear measure of how much the job was *worth*. Men were substantially more likely to measure their achievements against others and, as a result, to view money as a means of "keeping score." They took greater satisfaction from besting competitors and described themselves as motivated by opposition. They agreed with the statement, "I play to win."

These are clearly measures of worth that most organizations expect employees, especially those in senior positions, to hold. The grand bargain of the modern workplace rests on the exchange of time and skilled effort for financial reward. The greater the compensation and the more extensive the benefits, the more the job is assumed to be "worth." Position is valued because it is tied to compensation: the higher you go, the more you earn. Salary and position are thus *the* primary means that most organizations use to recognize individual achievement because these are the measures companies assume their employees will most value.

Financial rewards matter profoundly. They determine the quality of an employee's livelihood and his or her ability to support a family. Supporting oneself and one's family is the primary reason that most people work—and continue to do so even when they know that their work undermines them and their families (more on this later). But beyond just providing security and comfort, financial rewards also serve as a *symbolic* means of measuring an individual's success and defining where one stands in the pecking order. Placing a numeric value on contribution provides an abstract way of gauging worth, which is perceived as particularly satisfying by those who are motivated by competitive achievement.

Purely numerical valuations of worth assume a highly exaggerated form in companies where competition against others is both an expected behavior and a core cultural value. For example, Julie recalls seeing bonus checks at a major trading house cut in the amount of $1,000,001 during the time she worked there. Clearly, the extra dollar made no material difference in the lives of the people who received it. It was purely symbolic, a means of indicating that the recipients were more highly valued than those who received a mere $1,000,000 bonus. As such, it had meaning *only to someone who placed a high value on scorekeeping.*

Our Satisfaction Survey indicated that women tended to place a lower value on keeping score and took less intrinsic satisfaction than men in competitive achievement. Compensation was certainly important to the women in our survey; they expected to be paid fairly and they wanted to be paid well. But they were more likely to view compensation as a *means* to an end—providing a good life for themselves and their families— rather than as an end in itself.

The women in our study placed a high value on opportunities for social interaction and rated the quality of relationships they formed on the job as more satisfying than monetary rewards. They described themselves as preferring to cooperate rather than compete with colleagues. They were more likely than the men in the study to agree with the statement, "I will pick up the slack for others to assure that a project is successful." It was the *project* that mattered, in part because the project provided a vehicle for building relationships, and in part because they wanted to feel that their work served a larger purpose.

The women also placed a higher value than the men on work that enabled them to meet their domestic responsibilities. Because they were motivated both by what Steven Pinker terms intrinsic rewards (see chapter 2) and by the desire to provide support for their families, they valued work that did not expect or require what they deemed to be undue sacrifices in their domestic or personal lives. They sought congruence between their lives at work and their lives at home and were more likely than the men in the study to describe themselves as "striving to be the same person at work and at home." As a result, they enjoyed integrating the business and personal aspects of their lives. Like the speechwriter discussed in chapter 4, they sought to bring insights from home to work and vice versa rather than to compartmentalize their personal and business concerns.

The women also took satisfaction in meeting their own standards for performance instead of measuring their achievements against those of others. Winning was less important than accomplishing what they set out to achieve for themselves. This was the primary reason that competition did not stir or motivate them as strongly as it did the men. They valued the process, and as a result were less likely to view work within the context of a game.

The measures of satisfaction preferred by the women in our survey are counter to the culture of most organizations, particularly those in the private sector. They are not what companies expect employees to find rewarding. They do not fit the *vision* organizations have of what motivates people, inspires their loyalty, and spurs their best performance. And they may be out of sync with what many mainstream organizations assess to be a leadership temperament.

Many leaders over the last two decades have learned to speak the language of collaboration and teamwork. Yet the kind of collegiality the women in the survey prized is rarely as well compensated as the competitive spirit that seeks to score a win at every turn. For example, in most sales units, providing collaborative support to help a team member meet a goal is neither recognized nor rewarded. People are instead graded and ranked on their individual achievements.

The failure to collaborate rarely extracts a financial cost so long as an individual meets his or her numeric targets. Most organizations will reward even widely disliked or feared employees if they are seen as winners or producers. Because the damage these individuals do to the morale and loyalty of others in the company (and that of customers and clients) is often hard to quantify, their "winner-take-all" attitude is apt to be overvalued. This is especially true in highly competitive cultures whose leaders provide a template for the "who's-on-first" model.

Such organizations routinely pit employees against one another in an effort to spur competition, assigning comparative rank to achievements and grading performance on a rigorously numerical scale. As an extreme example, Jack Welch of GE gained fame for advocating that every employee's performance be ranked on a bell curve and that the entire bottom 10 percent be fired each year. The alleged purpose of this policy was to clear out the deadwood and keep employees motivated by the cold fear of being tagged as a "low potential."[3] At the zenith of Welch's influence, the 10-percent rule was widely copied, heralded as a "best practice" for organizations, and identified as a core tenet of the vaunted "Welch Way."

But such practices assume that performance is best measured against *how someone else is doing*. They also take for granted that fear and the desire to be better than someone else are the most effective spurs to performance. Yet since our survey found that women in fact prefer to measure themselves against their *own* standards, it is likely that female motivational triggers will be most powerfully engaged in organizations that give employees greater autonomy to set their own goals. These goals must, of course, be aligned with the organization's larger purpose. But reducing that purpose to numbers that can be plotted neatly on a graph is unlikely to spur authentic engagement.

Just as leaders in most organizations have learned to talk the language of collaboration, they have also learned to voice commitment to "work/life balance." Yet programs and policies developed to support this commitment are routinely abandoned or cut back when the organization comes under financial pressure and needs to adapt by cutting costs. This pattern suggests that organizations do not place a high value on such policies, viewing them as perhaps useful in times of plenty but not essential to morale, motivation, talent retention, or performance.

Companies faced with financial pressure are often unlikely to consider cutting compensation for the most highly paid employees; they assume that doing so would undermine performance and make it impossible to attract and retain talented people. This way of thinking is so ingrained that even companies that were bankrupted in the financial crisis defended using bailout funds to pay huge bonuses to the very employees who had led them to disaster on the grounds that doing so was required if they were to attract the best and the brightest.[4] The entire system in many companies is predicated on the presumption that the best people, the ones with the highest potential, are always motivated by the prospect of the largest possible financial rewards. Yet our results suggest that this may not necessarily be the best way to engage or inspire the loyalty of talented women.

Satisfaction and Daily Experience

One of the most significant satisfaction differentials to emerge from our survey is that women are more likely to assign value to their work based on the quality of their daily experience than on what their job implies for the progression of their careers.[5] The statistical evidence for this conclusion was particularly strong. For the men in our study, what a job might *lead to* held paramount importance. If they perceived it as a means for helping them ascend to a higher position, they were willing to sacrifice the quality of their lives; they deemed the abstract goal of future success to be "worth it." By contrast, the women placed a higher value on work that they found enjoyable and rewarding on a daily basis. They took satisfaction from the texture of their everyday experience rather than from seeing the present as a stepping stone to the future.

This finding echoed in updated form what Sally found while doing research for *The Female Advantage*.[6] In benchmarking her study of female leaders against Henry Mintzberg's classic survey of male executives, Sally noted that Mintzberg's men in that earlier study paid little attention to the quality of their daily experience.[7] As she observed, "Mintzberg's managers were focused on the completion of tasks and the achievement of goals, rather than on the actual doing of the tasks themselves." As a result, they barely *noticed* the texture of their lives.[8]

Mintzberg believed that the single-minded pursuit of what came next made it difficult for the men he studied to live in the present moment. Their eyes were trained on the heights they hoped to achieve or the depths they hoped to avoid. He also found that his subjects' instrumental view of work and relationships deprived their lives of richness and depth. Finally, he felt their emphasis on what came next—what a job would lead to rather than the rewards it offered—made them prone to feeling empty and futile if their hopes did not materialize.[9]

The women in our survey were more likely than the men to take satisfaction in the performance of their daily tasks. They were therefore less likely to see these activities as instrumental; they viewed them as having value in and of themselves. Again, this is contrary to the culture of most organizations. Most companies operate on the presumption that people will ignore the quality of their daily lives in exchange for the promise of future achievement. The future is presumed to provide the carrot, as it did for Mintzberg's men, while the fear of failure is presumed to provide the stick. But our research suggests that this may be a poor way to engage the passions and loyalty of many talented women.

Julie's client, Jennifer, gives a clear demonstration of how the future fallacy can work differently with women. Jennifer had been with her company, one of the world's largest consumer products firms, for twenty years and considered herself fiercely loyal. She had climbed the ranks because she was trusted, well-liked, unusually smart, and was considered a tireless worker.

Jennifer enjoyed her position as an executive vice president running two major divisions. She was surprised when the CEO asked her to become the company's chief financial officer (at the client's request, her name has been changed). She did not feel she had the technical background the position required and preferred the daily satisfactions of leading her team to the challenges the new position would represent.

But the CEO was eager for her to take the job; the company's executive bench was thin and the manager who had been groomed for the position had left the company. The CEO promised to give Jennifer all the support she needed to meet her responsibilities, and noted that accepting the position would put her in line to succeed him when he retired.

Seeking to get up to speed on the technical aspects of her role as CFO, Jennifer drove herself and her team almost 24/7 for nearly a year. Given that kind of pressure, it was hardly surprising that her reputation for being a great boss and an inspiring team leader began to suffer. As her relationships within the company began to fray, she felt more and more exposed; being the only woman on the executive team added to her sense of isolation.

Having so little time for her family also made her question what she was doing with her life; she wondered how being CFO fit with what she perceived as her larger purpose. Her high position afforded her little pleasure because she was too frazzled to enjoy the texture of her days. As she says, "I felt so much responsibility for my job and seemed to take things harder than the men around me. I was also miserable because I was losing touch with what had always motivated me as a leader—developing and inspiring my people."

In the spring of 2008, as the economic crisis unfolded, Jennifer prepared for a difficult meeting with an investor her company was seeking to bring in on a deal, working herself almost to exhaustion to get ready. Several members of the executive team who were scheduled to accompany her had expertise in the arcane fields in which Jennifer had little background, so she felt confident she could rely on them to cover technical questions.

The investor started things off with a series of unexpected questions, mostly relating to the broader financial environment. As pressure mounted during the meeting, it became clear to her that several team members—including the CEO—were too panicked and paralyzed to respond. Jennifer had anticipated that they would be available to back her up, but now found that she had to fend for herself. The fact that colleagues she had known for two decades failed to rally behind her served as a wake-up call.

The meeting changed Jennifer's attitude toward herself and her work. She became more cognizant of the toll her commitment was taking on herself, her family, and her team. She began pushing back against what she considered unreasonable demands and stopped giving herself a hard time. She recognized that she took her own contribution to the company more seriously than her colleagues did, and she started to develop a tougher hide.

As a result, she became more comfortable articulating her own values and stopped trying to adapt to her senior colleagues' vision of what really mattered. As she noted, "getting to the top slot in the company is the be-all and end-all for most of these guys. I used to feel that I *should* feel that way, but now I've realized that life's too short. I want to enjoy my work, not live for future status. It's just not worth it."

Worth and stress

In January 2009, Dave Krasne, a former banker at Merrill Lynch, contributed an editorial to the *New York Times* about the culture of the bonus. Krasne noted that the people he worked with on Wall Street believed they deserved what others might consider wildly disproportionate compensation because of the hours their companies required them to work. Only huge sums, he wrote, were believed to "justify the days on end of working into the wee hours, the months on end without a single day off, the never-ending 'fire drills'—when a client wanted something and wanted it now, whether it was 7 p.m. or 7 a.m.—that kept the stress and adrenaline levels high."[10]

Krasne perfectly describes the pressure and intensity that began to characterize much of the workplace starting in the mid-1990s. As 24/7 technologies spread and the global economy intensified competition, people found themselves working longer and harder than they had since the early days of the industrial era, and in sectors far beyond the rarefied precincts of investment banking. As businesses sought to operate more leanly, employers began demanding that their employees ramp up their efforts as soon as they completed demanding projects. The very notion of downtime began to disappear.

Though the pace struck many as unsustainable, most had no choice but to keep slogging away. For Krasne's bankers, unprecedented bonuses were viewed as offering appropriate compensation for unremitting effort. And given the grand bargain of the modern workplace—time in exchange for money— why *wouldn't* more time simply translate into more money?

But women weren't necessarily buying into this logic. In retrospect, it makes sense that women's ascent into senior management positions began to stall in the early 1990s, the very period when workplace demands were becoming more intense.[11] The unceasing and exhausting pace often hit women harder because they were likely to be working a "second shift" at home. So it is hardly surprising that some of the most talented women would respond by leaving their organizations or taking themselves off the leadership track.

As companies recognized the nature of this conundrum, many sought to stem the exodus of talented women by offering flextime and work-from-home opportunities aimed at supporting a work/life balance. Workshops and seminars on achieving balance became staples at women's conferences, though in some instances this only seemed to add to the pressure. For example, Sally remembers a corporate networking retreat held over a weekend—a dubious innovation in itself—in early 2000 that offered a session called "The Balanced Woman" at seven o'clock on a Sunday morning!

Yet our study suggests that the pace and intensity of work is an issue for women not only because of their multiple responsibilities but also because of the value they place on the quality of their days.[12] The measures of satisfaction preferred by the women in the survey are particularly at odds with the "all-work-all-the-time" culture that began to spread in the 1990s. Valuing daily experience over abstract measures and future prospects, women are, not surprisingly, more apt to *notice* when the quality of their lives is declining. Unlike Krasne's investment bankers, women have often been reluctant to sacrifice their ability to enjoy their daily lives in exchange for ever larger amounts of money. Again, this goes against the prevailing business culture, which assumes that time is always unquestionably *worth it* if enough money is offered in exchange.

Women may also have been less willing to consider this exchange to be worth it because they experience the stress and adrenaline to which Krasne refers in a different way. For example, Dr. Amy Arnsten, professor of neurobiology at Yale, notes that hormonal differences between male and female animals modulate the degree of stress individuals experience and determine their ability to cope with its effects.[13] She finds that females are often more susceptible to stress because estrogen slows the recovery time between stress responses, while males require more stimulation in order to remain engaged.

Extrapolating this research into the human realm, Arnsten speculates that, although females may function better in less stressful conditions, men require more stimulation. Or, as she observes, "Males seem more likely to be bored, while females are more likely to be stressed."[14]

Arnsten has developed a useful tool for mapping differences in how males and females experience stress, which she calls the "boredom/stress continuum" (see figure below). It takes the form of an inverted U.

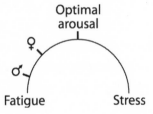

In the lower left quadrant, brain waves in the prefrontal cortex reflect a state of fatigue and boredom; someone in this state is difficult to motivate and is easily distracted. As the curve rises along the left, the brain becomes more active. The top of the curve represents a state of optimal arousal—what some psychologists call *flow*—in which an individual feels relaxed but also alert and fully engaged. But as engagement becomes more intense, pressure erodes, and the curve accelerates down into a state of stress.[15]

If, as Arnsten's research suggests, males start out at a lower point on the curve, it makes sense that they would be more likely than women to feel bored and would require more stimulation to be engaged. Because women start out at a higher point on the curve, they require less motivation for arousal, but are also more easily tipped into stress.

We believe these findings have huge implications for women and for organizations. Most companies invest a lot of effort in motivating employees, trying to push them to ever higher levels of performance either by issuing threats (competitive statistical rankings may be used for this purpose) or by piling on the rewards. Such motivators are seen as essential to performance, which is not surprising given that organizations have until fairly recently been focused on engaging the talents of men. But what has been presumed to work in the past may not provide the optimal way to retain talented women.

While organizations focus resources on trying to motivate their people, few expend much effort in trying to mitigate stress. Yet the research we've cited suggests that this approach may in fact undermine women. Diverse organizations seeking to get the best from women as well as men must put more effort into building cultures in which people feel neither bored nor stressed but rather *valued*.

Evidence from Women Entrepreneurs

Over the last two decades, the number of women choosing to become entrepreneurs has steadily risen. Women now start their own businesses at a faster rate than men.[16] Looking at what drives their decisions can give us a better understanding of what talented women consider "worth it."

In *How She Does It*, her insightful study of female entrepreneurs, Margaret Heffernan offers clues that supplement and support what we found in our Satisfaction Survey.[17] The women Heffernan profiled, who had left mainstream organizations in order to found their own companies, were not motivated primarily by money, although money was certainly important to them, especially since a significant proportion were primary breadwinners in their families.

Instead, Heffernan's subjects sought greater flexibility, more autonomy, a higher degree of work/life integration, and more scope for building strong relationships. Because they wanted more control over their own time, they sought to build cultures that avoided putting what they considered "pointless pressure" on themselves and on people who worked for them. Many stated specifically that they wanted to create nurturing environments in which talented women—women who shared their values—could thrive. They believed that doing so would give them a competitive advantage in attracting these women and would make work a lot more fun for everyone involved.

A number of the women Heffernan studied were explicitly inspired by the desire to build workplace cultures different from those in companies they had worked in. One successful entrepreneur, a former petroleum industry executive, summed it up: "I learned everything I needed to know about how *not* to motivate people at my last company. So when I started my business, I tried to do the opposite of what they had done. I wanted to create an environment in which people felt valued. I figured that was the best way to keep great people engaged."

Although Heffernan did her research during a period when many entrepreneurs were trying to build companies as fast as possible, she found few successful female entrepreneurs who were motivated by this goal. As one said, "Why would I want to do that? I built this company so I'd have a place *I* would love to work." Given her motivation, making a fortune and cashing out would make no sense.

Heffernan quotes Nancy Peretsman, a media investor with Allen & Company, who is approached regularly with entrepreneurial proposals. She says, "Guys come in here saying, 'my goal is to make X amount of money,' or 'this place will be worth $200 million in X number of years.' They're totally driven by financial returns, by numbers." By contrast, the female entrepreneurs who approach Peretsman have a broader focus. "They see money as a product of success. But it's not the only product."

The women Heffernan studied were building businesses for the long term in order to satisfy a range of goals and ambitions. Because they sought to create enterprises that would support and sustain their families and employees, they were not particularly driven by the desire to become "big, big, big." The texture of the lives they were able to construct by going into business for themselves mattered more than purely financial measures of success.

Heffernan's subjects were diligent about knowing the numbers, but they did not judge their success based on their size. Their preoccupation with providing a superior experience for clients and customers made them skeptical of rapid growth. Because of this—and because their experience with out-of-control corporate pressures made many of them avid for control and flexibility—the female entrepreneurs Heffernan studied tended to be fiscally conservative and resistant to assuming a lot of debt. In this, they provided a stark contrast to the broader entrepreneurial culture that developed during the boom years leading up to the financial crisis, when taking on debt to finance expansion and drive up the numbers before selling out became routine.

The values women entrepreneurs bring to their business may provide a key to understanding a paradox that lies at the heart of the growth of female-owned enterprises. On one hand, companies owned by women are twice as likely to stay in business as those owned by men, while those owned by women of color are *four times* more likely to survive.[18] Female entrepreneurs also have a higher rate of loan repayment. Yet women's businesses remain for the most part small when compared with those owned by men, in part because they are vastly undercapitalized when compared with companies founded by men.[19] Less than 10 percent of venture capital goes to women-owned firms, and those firms that do receive funding receive much smaller amounts.

Conventional wisdom has attributed this gap to the persistence of old boy networks, and a male preference for lending money to other men. Heffernan, who worked in venture capital, sees the problem as rooted in a lack of imagination rather than in hostility or prejudice. She points out that many male venture capitalists have almost no experience dealing with women and don't know how to judge what they bring to the table. She also notes that women who start capital-intensive enterprises—for example, in the technology sector, which has a higher proportion of men—are also more likely to raise outside money.

Given that many women business owners report being motivated by the desire to gain greater autonomy and control over their lives, however, it naturally follows that they would be less avid in pursuing outside investors, who would inevitably assume a large measure of control. A company carrying a lot of leverage can hardly guarantee that either its owners or its employees will have the scope to pursue flexibility, work/life integration, a high quality of daily experience, and strong relationships, while quickly earning a high return on investment. Even if a founder wants to put the numbers within the context of broader goals, investors may not find this agenda compelling. It is therefore not surprising that female entrepreneurs often choose to grow at a deliberate pace.

CHAPTER SIX

The Social Fabric

J ust as what we notice determines what we value, so what we value shapes our picture of how the world should be. This ethical dimension forms the third element of our vision. Unlike noticing and valuing, both of which occur within ourselves, in our minds and our hearts, the third component of our vision is manifest in our actions.

Our daily actions have real power when they serve the purpose of our larger vision, providing a link between what we are doing now, at this present moment, and what we most profoundly want to achieve in the world. Being clear about this connection—being able to articulate how our actions serve our larger vision—gives us a sense of purpose and inspiration and provides us with a yardstick against which to measure our decisions.

Aligning our actions with our larger vision can be challenging for women working in organizations. As we've seen, traditional assumptions about what's "worth it" in the workplace do not necessarily compel women's deepest engagement. Nor are women's strategic perceptions always recognized. Our Satisfaction Survey, along with the other research discussed in chapter 5, make clear that many women tend to locate meaning in social relationships rather than in competitive rankings. So it's not surprising that organizational goals and mission statements focused on numerical measures often strike women as hollow.

Sally saw a perfect example of this disjunction when she participated in a retreat for senior women at Company A, one of the world's leading medical suppliers in 2004. Company A was a widely admired blue chip whose bottom line and reputation had suffered while it was pursuing an aggressive policy of acquisition. Several of the companies it bought turned out to have hidden ethical or balance sheet problems. This created pressure on Company A to recoup losses by increasing demands on employees to constantly justify or cut costs, which in turn led to a decline in morale. People were exhausted by trying to continually put out fires and were dismayed to see their company—previously a perennial on most-admired lists—the subject of negative attention.

It was in this environment that three hundred senior women from various operating divisions gathered for a retreat at corporate headquarters. They spent most of the session listening to panelists and outside speakers sharing lessons they had learned or research they had done. The program culminated in a presentation by a member of the nine-person corporate executive committee. His participation was billed as an indication of how much Company A valued its up-and-coming women and honored their vital role in making it a great company.

The presenter opened his PowerPoint to a slide that proclaimed the executive committee's mantra: *We are committed to 6 percent yearly revenue growth for the next five years.*

He then proceeded with a series of slides showing a robust future for the company predicated on rapid growth, both geographically and in terms of product lines. He demonstrated that this would be achieved in part by expanding the company's acquisitions. He graphed the costs various divisions would have to absorb to free up funds for continued expansion and offered charts comparing competitor growth with Company A's projections.

The presentation concluded with a simple screen that read, "One Company: One Vision," accompanied by a voice-over chorus reciting these words. As the sound faded, the executive spoke.

"These next years are going to be *very* demanding," he said. "But if we keep focused on our purpose, we will achieve 30 percent growth in five years. This will put us ahead of our largest competitor for the first time in eighteen years!"

The applause came, but hardly at the crescendo the executive seemed to expect. A woman who managed one of the company's largest divisions rose to ask the first question.

"My people are already working sixty hours a week and they're losing motivation," she said. "Am I supposed to tell them this will go on for the next five years?"

The presenter replied that her unit might need to use its time more efficiently and help them by instilling a sense of commitment.

Several of the remaining questions shared a skeptical tone, but the presenter's confidence in the motivating power of his message remained undiminished. In closing, he noted that transformation required a lot of hard work but declared that the dream he had outlined would be worth the effort. "I'm challenging you: let's shoot for the moon!"

Later, the conference planners gathered for dinner in a nearby hotel to discuss how the day had gone.

"I don't get it," said one of the women. "Isn't rapid acquisition what got us into all this trouble in the first place? Does he really think we wouldn't notice that?"

"He talked as if acquisitions come without any costs," agreed another. "We can't inspire our people or instill a sense of commitment if we try to pretend this isn't an issue."

"Why is talking about 30 percent growth supposed to be so meaningful?" a division operating head asked. "Is growth our ultimate purpose? Don't we need to look at what growth *means* for our customers and our people? Or is the whole idea just to be able to say we grew 30 percent?"

Although the women were concerned about the consequences of a continued frantic pace, their larger objection was to the executive's strategic premise, which he framed simply as rapid growth achieved by means of continued acquisition. The women knew their company had to keep growing—a market economy does not tolerate stagnation—but they viewed growth as a *means* to an end rather than an end in itself. Hearing growth itself described as a vision, a purpose, a dream, and a commitment raised for them the inevitable question: *Growth in the service of what?*

The Metaphor of the Game

The author and consultant Pat Heim has described incidents such as Sally witnessed at the conference as classic examples of gender miscommunication, the result of men and women using different words to mean the same things or using the same words in different ways.[1] Heim notes that women often get tagged as poor team players because they ask probing questions during strategic discussions. Women may assume that whoever is presenting a plan is interested in hearing what others have to say about it. In fact, Heim notes that the presenter may simply want nothing more than for someone to respond, "What a great idea! I'm on board!"

This dynamic seemed to be operating at Company A's retreat. The speaker had arrived with the mission of firing up the women, but had instead managed to stir their resistance by advocating a course of action with which many disagreed. Although he presented it in a language that evoked vision and purpose, his focus on purely competitive measures did not strike the women as sufficiently inspiring or strategic.

Why did the presenter miss his mark so badly?

One reason is that the metaphor that informed his presumptions was the metaphor of the game. The game has provided one of the dominant ways that people understand and speak about business for most of the last century. It is reflected in the pervasive use of sports language to describe both activities and purpose: *we need a Hail Mary pass; let's hit it out of the bleachers; take your shot; win one for the Gipper.*

It's not clear that game metaphors—and they *are* metaphors, for business is not a game, however much those engaged in it might like it to be—provide a particularly effective means of motivating women. Until very recently, few women had much experience with team sports. This historical situation is changing as social innovations such as Title IX have substantially boosted girls' participation in organized games.[2] But sports analogies can still seem incomplete or beside the point to many women.

Our Satisfaction Survey found that women are less likely

than men to agree with statements such as, "I play to win," "The tougher the game, the harder I play," and "Money for me is just a way of keeping score."[3] They were more likely to agree with statements such as "I choose work that is useful to society and others," "I strive to be the same person at work and at home," and "If I help someone, I don't necessarily expect anything in return." The first group of statements accurately describe someone engaged in playing a game, while the second group do not. Similarly, the research noted in chapter 5 showing the primacy women place on relationships at work does not accord with the attitude in sports, in which bonding primarily serves the purpose of the game.

Games are strictly bounded; life is not. Games have clear rules; life is subject to ceaseless reinterpretation. Games are discrete events that matter in the short term; life plays out over the years. Games have clear winners and losers: as the football coach Vince Lombardi famously observed, winning is *the only thing* that matters in a game. What happens in one game also has no impact upon what happens in the next: whether you're playing football or solitaire, each game offers the possibility of a fresh and unfettered start. As Leonard Greenhalgh, professor of management at Dartmouth, observes, "The history and future of an ongoing relationship between contestants is irrelevant in sports."[4] This is not true in organizations.[5]

Greenhalgh, who has studied gender differences in negotiating styles, believes the persistence of game metaphors in business can actually undermine men's effectiveness over the long term. He notes that those who set transactions in a win-or-lose frame tend to undervalue the larger context and the need for building relationships. Focusing too much on a "winning" outcome can result in a competitor feeling burned, which may have a negative impact on future negotiations. Greenhalgh also finds that the metaphor of "playing by the rules" can encourage a legalistic frame of mind that devalues the importance of trust and increases the tendency to litigate disputes.

It's ironic that women, who resist the kind of game metaphors that Greenhalgh views as inherently short term, are often viewed as lacking in strategic vision. For example, a study of multinational companies by the Madrid-based Washington Quality Group (WQG) found that women's bosses rated them lower than women rated themselves on visionary capacity, defined as the ability to see the future and consider the larger picture.[6] In every other measure of performance, women *under*-assessed their own performance when compared not only with their bosses but with their peers and with direct reports. By contrast, men *over*-assessed their own performance in every criteria when compared with the same groups.

We can assume from this that the women in the survey either did, in fact, lack vision—which seems unlikely since it was one area in which they perceived themselves as having strength—or that they were not doing an effective job of communicating the strength of their vision upward in the organization.

The WQG data also showed that women were perceived as lacking vision *in relative proportion* to the skill they were perceived to bring to relationships. That is, those who were best with people were deemed to be particularly lacking in long-term or big picture skills. Men seen as visionary, by contrast, tended to be viewed as less skilled with people. Given that industrial culture has traditionally viewed toughness as an essential element of leadership, and that leadership is seen as synonymous with vision, it makes sense that those perceived as proficient in skills routinely described as "soft" might routinely be under-assessed when it comes to vision.

Maintaining the social fabric has, throughout history, been perceived as the work of women. As a result, women have developed a sensitivity to the nuance of relationships. As the WQG data suggests, this sensitivity is not necessarily seen as a leadership quality. It has therefore often been viewed as a kind of frill in the rough and tumble of organizations—nice, but beside the point and expendable during periods when pressure grows intense.

But as organizations grow more weblike, more dependent upon relationships and the nurturance of talent, the strategic nature of tending the social fabric becomes more apparent. The capacity to integrate social skills into a larger vision offers women a way to move beyond outmoded dichotomies between big-picture thinking and the care and maintenance of relationships. In a world of webs, the ability to see decisions in a larger human context becomes an essential, and profoundly strategic, advantage.

Johnna's Story

The benefits of linking strategy to the social fabric can be seen in the story of Johnna Torsone, executive vice president and chief human resources officer at Pitney Bowes. Johnna joined the Fortune 500 company in 1990, with a background in labor and employment law. Future CEO Mike Critelli, who hired her, was impressed by Johnna's ability to ground corporate-level decisions in a broader human context. He says, "She has an unusual capacity for noticing people's behavior on an everyday level and integrating it into the strategic discussion. This has made her the conscience of the organization at the leadership level."[7]

Johnna's capabilities proved a particular asset in 1996, when the company's senior management team was considering changing its executive compensation program. The then-prevailing view among investors, compensation consultants, and governance experts was that companies needed to align executive and shareholder interest by increasing executive stock holdings. Awarding larger stock-based compensation, especially in the form of supplemental option grants, was also viewed as the best way to encourage innovative thinking and spur competitive performance. Because Pitney Bowes's original business of marketing postage meters was rapidly expanding into the development of broader "mailstream" solutions, the senior team saw a need to send a strong message that the new environment would require executives to focus on accelerated growth.

Johnna stood alone in opposing significantly expanded stock-option grants. In senior team meetings, she articulated her reasons. She believed that dangling outsized rewards in front of people would lead to dysfunctional behavior by spurring even cautious executives to take risks that could compromise the company's performance and reputation in the longer term. She also believed that granting extra stock options to a handful of executives was inconsistent with the company's egalitarian and team-oriented culture, which had been an asset in aligning the organization around common goals. Critelli says, "She made her points very strongly at our leadership meetings. But there was a lot of pushback, a lot of pressure to go for it. The executive team saw expanding options as a bold strategic move."

Because of Johnna's strong advocacy, the senior leadership team decided to test the waters. It would offer supplemental options in one small business that was part of the company's financial services division before rolling them out as a matter of corporate policy. The leadership of this unit had a reputation for being very cautious in how it valued and acquired assets and in refusing to bid on portfolios that competitors eagerly sought out. It thus exemplified the risk-averse approach that the company was trying to change.

As soon as the supplemental options were offered, behavior in the unit shifted. Executives formerly known for their caution began changing the parameters they used to guide cost-benefit analysis. Eager to increase their own worth on paper by raising the net number of contracts they serviced, members of the unit began to bid on business they wouldn't even have considered in the past. The potential payoff for exercising a large number of options became the prime driver of the division's behavior, the rationale against which decisions were measured.

As a result, a division that had always recorded steady and profitable growth began incurring substantial loses. Within a few years, Pitney Bowes decided to sell the business. But the experiment had served its purpose. Confronted with evidence of behavioral changes brought about by offering large options, senior leadership accepted Johnna's judgment and decided against offering them.

In retrospect, it's easy to see why offering huge pools of stock to reward performance would lead employees to take excessive risks. It's also easy to see how these options would end up diluting the value of corporate shares once stock price inflation began to slow. But in the mid-1990s, the granting of what were popularly known as "mega options" was viewed as a cutting-edge practice, a strategic necessity in a highly competitive new world. Pitney Bowes was able to buck this influential trend because Johnna Torsone took responsibility for articulating what she noticed and linking it to her strategic understanding. As Mike Critelli notes, she had "the moral courage to stand against the tide, to speak her mind in a way that compelled attention."

Johnna viewed her company as a social as well as a financial entity. This gave her an understanding of human motivation. She was able to use it to build a constituency for policy based on her vision of what the company could and should be. Resisting conventional wisdom, she helped keep leadership grounded in what had traditionally been best about the company's culture.

In doing so, she was able to move beyond the time-honored female role of Cassandra. Rather than simply sounding the warning against an impending disaster she was powerless to avert, she took responsible action to forestall its negative consequences. By advocating and building a constituency for what she saw and valued, Johnna was able to move her company onto a different path.

She was also able to move beyond the paralysis and frustration experienced by the women in the example of Company A. Although those senior women were astute in observing the weakness in the plan presented at their conference, they failed to use what they observed to influence the larger conversation. They *noticed* a problem, but they did not translate their critique into action.

As a result, they accepted their company's compartmentalized view of their own leadership potential. Rather than seeing the women's leadership initiative as a resource for expanding the company's vision, they accepted it as a stand-alone effort—worthy but of little strategic value. This left the women demoralized and questioning whether their contribution was "worth it." It also deprived Company A of the true potential that diversity offers.

PART III

Profiting from the Female Vision

CHAPTER SEVEN

Acting on Your Vision

W hen the female vision remains untapped, both women and organizations suffer. Women are unable to translate their best observations into action. What they see remains locked within them, and their connections with others can feel shallow and inauthentic as a result. What should be a source of power becomes a source of isolation and frustration.

Without the female vision, organizations also lose power. They undermine the full potential of their talent base. They diminish the capacity of their people to make balanced decisions. They undermine creativity and reduce the potential for real collaboration. They remain one dimensional in a multidimensional world.

In order for this to change, women must take the initiative. They can't wait for organizations to start valuing what they see. Women themselves must build a market for what they offer by teaching their companies to recognize the power and value of the female vision. In this way they can create the change they seek.

Our research, as well as Julie's many years of working with clients, suggests that acting on your vision requires taking four specific steps: articulating your vision, enlisting allies, holding yourself accountable, and remaining fully present.

Articulate Your Vision

You start by being as clear as you can about what you see and communicating it in a way that your organization can understand and value. This requires developing a story that explains what you notice, why it matters, and what it can mean for people in your company in the years ahead. You must own this story, believing and valuing it in your heart, and conveying it in your actions with fortitude and persistence.

Communicating the value of what you see does not mean simply putting it out there and hoping people will find it persuasive. It means spelling it out so that others perceive it as serving their interests, their goals, their future hopes. Your vision must also reflect how people really view the organization—what they like about it, what they perceive as distinctive, how they understand its purpose. The more closely you articulate the alignment between what you see and what the organization authentically *is*, the greater your chances of persuading others to see your point of view.

Once you've thought through the implications of what you notice and value, you need to frame your vision in the language of benefit. If you are in a service role, you must show how your vision can improve the quality or delivery of a service, and you must specify the concrete outcomes that will result. If you are in a sales role, you must articulate how what you see can help achieve better results, by either expanding the pool of potential buyers or creating customer loyalty that produces higher profits or lower costs. If you are in strategic planning, you must describe how the policy or practice you envision will improve your organization's ability to adapt to specific and foreseeable future trends.

Julie's client Abby, the director of recruiting at one of New York's most prestigious law firms, was skilled in articulating her vision and connecting it to what was best in her firm's culture. Abby told a clear and detailed story about what she valued in her company and then used it as a vehicle for reinforcing those values. Her story centered on her firm's long tradition of collegiality, its preference for developing well-rounded partners and associates who treated one another with respect. Abby believed this tradition was an extraordinary asset, both internally because it made her company a great place to work, and externally because it inspired client loyalty. It also fit with her personal vision of how an organization should operate and function.

But Abby was also aware that the mainstream legal marketplace perceived the value of collegiality to be in decline. She watched competitors fiercely pursue lawyers who had gold-plated resumes but flagrantly bad interpersonal skills.

She says, "There are and there always will be top-tier firms that hire brilliant lawyers. But there are fewer and fewer such firms where the lawyers are a pleasure to work with. In the heat of the hiring season, it's tempting for the hiring committee to be swayed by a candidate's great credentials and/or family pedigree, and to overlook his or her more human qualities. But overvaluing sheer brilliance can lead to problems."

Abby believed it was her job to push back against the one-dimensional definition of legal talent that was becoming current in the market and to put her considerable skills into the service of furthering this goal. She *noticed* when the applicant with great credentials was rude to her staff or treated service people like underlings, and she was fearless in articulating the specific ways such people could undermine her firm in the long term. She kept a running file on the long-term bottom line value that collegial behavior produced and kept tabs on the costs of hiring go-it-alone star performers.

She says, "I constantly sought to show that *no* amount of talent can trump lack of courtesy or repair the damage done by an arrogant self-centered personality. And I made my case in terms that the partners in the firm would value."

The thoroughness with which she owned her vision gave her such credibility that the partners refused to hire anyone who did not pass "the Abby test."

Like Johnna Torsone in chapter 6, Abby was able to help her organization avoid falling prey to a popular business trend by appealing to what she most valued in the organization's culture. Johnna drew on Pitney Bowes's egalitarianism to make the case against outsized bonuses; Abby drew on her firm's reputation for collegiality to push back against the legal profession's growing tendency to define "high potential" in narrow or highly statistical terms rather than to look at the broader human picture.

Both Johnna and Abby created a receptive market for what they noticed and valued because of the consistency of their vision and their ability to set it in the context of a larger organizational story. Their commitment carried force and made them credible representatives for a distinctive point of view. Although both understood that the bottom line is never all that matters, they addressed bottom-line concerns in order to sell their vision. By taking responsibility for articulating what they saw, they released energy—their own and that of people around them.

Enlist Allies

The strongest, most well-articulated vision will have little effect on your organization if you don't enlist allies to support your view. Allies are people who are willing to listen, who try to help you when you ask, who give you feedback and explain your cause when you're not in the room. Allies give you inside information and explain political motivations you may have overlooked.

Allies are different from friends in that your relationship with them always serves a specific purpose. You are trying to accomplish something and your ally has a motive in helping you; there's a principle of mutual self-interest at work. The relationship is strategic; its purpose is to leverage power. You don't need to have a lot in common with an ally—you don't even necessarily need to enjoy one another's company—but you do need to trust one another.

Although women are often great at building relationships, they are not always great at creating allies because they can be uncomfortable using relationships to achieve specific ends. For example, our Satisfaction Survey, cited in chapter 5, found that men are more likely to enjoy workplace relationships that serve a transactional purpose, whereas women tend to value relationships at work for their own sake.[1] Similarly, Sally's research with professional service firms indicated that women often hesitated to ask colleagues for support because they feared being perceived as using others for their own purposes.

As we've seen, women's tending and befriending behaviors give them emotional resilience and decrease their susceptibility to stress. This provides them with many advantages. Yet the value women place on building relationships for their own sake can hinder them when it comes to leveraging relationships or using them to achieve specific ends. By thinking in terms of friendship rather than reciprocal advantages in cases where such advantages could be useful, women can undermine their power and their capacity to achieve their vision.

The executive coaching process often involves doing interviews and getting feedback from people within the organization about the leadership skills of the individual being coached. During one such session, Julie asked a senior executive in a financial services company for advice she could pass on to help a female client who reported to him.

He said, "I would tell her to spend more time sharing information with colleagues that she knows will help her in an explicit way. This will build up the amount of social capital she has at her disposal and give credits she can draw on when she needs to get things done." He noted that in his experience, men seemed more comfortable than women with the *quid pro quo* implicit in such exchanges.

Once they accept the value of leverage, women can benefit by putting their relationship skills to work building allies in a conscious and deliberate way. Julie's client Anne Cartwright, the executive vice president of a wealth management company, is an example. Anne felt that her firm should be doing a better job of assigning work to associates and should use these assignments to develop talent in a more deliberate and thoughtful way. She knew she had the skills and insights needed to help manage this process, but she was stymied in her efforts to get the company to reevaluate how it assigned work because she didn't have allies to support her. Anne had been so focused on becoming an expert in her functional field and providing great service to her clients that she had neglected to build social capital within the firm.

In order to achieve her vision, Anne needed to develop broader, stronger, and more robust relationships. She sat down and made a list of all the people in the organization she needed to know better. She made notes on who had influence with whom, who had important connections, and who could be instrumental in shaping her future. She thought very deliberately about what she might be able to offer each person on the list, in terms of information, introductions, small favors, or support. Having always been superb at providing client service, Anne now found herself adapting these skills to serve internal clients.

She decided to share her plan with her boss. She told him precisely what she was doing and asked his advice about opportunities that might help her get more connected. She had resisted doing so at first, fearing that he'd think she was wasting time. Instead, he interpreted her efforts as strengthening *him* by extending his own connections inside the company.

To keep herself on track, Anne developed a spreadsheet she called "last time met" and put it on her desktop. It helped her keep track of who she had reached out to and who she needed to contact. It also provided a graphic representation of her growing network, a map that helped her identify where she needed to work on vertical relationships and where she needed to work with peers.

Finally, Anne made an effort to draw more attention in the firm to her own work with clients in order to build her credibility with colleagues. She realized that she had always just assumed that the other partners knew she was doing an outstanding job, and had shied away from the effort of keeping them informed. As she abandoned self-sabotaging modesty, she recognized that her colleagues valued knowing about her client skills. Some began to use her as a sounding board about client relationships. By consciously leveraging others as a resource, Anne was thus able to provide them with a resource as well.

Hold Yourself Accountable

Once you have articulated your vision and enlisted allies, you need a plan of action, and you need to make a commitment to follow through on it. Many people are good at drawing up plans but fewer are skilled at identifying the resources they will need to see their plans through to the end. Follow-through can be especially difficult for women who may feel isolated in their organizations or may be accustomed to having the value of what they say discounted. When they feel unsupported, women can grow discouraged, deciding the task they've set themselves is too great, or letting daily demands fritter their energy away.

To avoid these common traps, you need a system for holding yourself accountable to act upon what you see and for developing the support you will need when the going gets tough.

Two techniques are particularly useful in assuring persistence: identifying an accountability partner and working with a peer coach.

Accountability Partner

An accountability partner is someone in your organization whom you see on a daily (or almost daily) basis and who understands what you are trying to do. Your accountability partner does not necessarily need to know the big picture—how you conceive of your ultimate vision. But he or she does need sufficient information about the specifics of what you are attempting to change to give you regular feedback about how well your actions support your goals.

An accountability partner is a one-way relationship. You don't necessarily exchange critiques. Instead, you invite someone to help keep you honest with yourself. The point is not to take all the advice you get from this partner but rather to add an additional perspective so you can identify when you need to make course corrections.

Having an accountability partner can enhance your self-awareness by forcing you to see how your actions are perceived by others. Self-awareness is one of the keys to acting on your vision. Visionary leaders know what they want to achieve, but they also know themselves and have a clear picture of how their actions affect others. A study at the Center for Creative Leadership found that self-awareness is *the* primary quality that distinguishes successful leaders.[2] Authenticity requires self-awareness because self-awareness keeps things real. This is very difficult to achieve on your own.

Your accountability partner does not need to be your

friend. Rachel, one of Julie's clients, picked her archenemy in the organization to be her accountability partner. She figured his perspective would provide a bracing antidote to her own perceptions about how effectively she was working to achieve her objectives. He was stunned when she asked him to hold her accountable for delivering on her plan. Although the observations he shared were often painful, Rachel persisted through the awkwardness and got an eye-opening view of both her strengths and her weaknesses.

After a few weeks, Rachel realized that her former enemy was now actively engaged in trying to make her successful. She was not only gaining valuable insights into her own behavior, she had also turned a skeptic into a supporter. In the process of holding herself accountable, Rachel had enlisted an ally.

Peer Coach

Another way to develop self-awareness and hold yourself accountable is to employ the simple but powerful practice of peer coaching. A peer coach is different than an accountability partner in three essential ways. Peer coaching is a reciprocal arrangement in which peers provide help for one another. It focuses on specific actions rather than general observations—it's more "did you do this?" than "how am I doing?" Peer coaching also serves personal development needs in addition to addressing specific goals, although it employs a highly tactical approach to doing so.

A peer coach can be someone either inside or outside the organization. Choosing a close friend can be helpful, though the friend should not be someone for whom you can do no wrong. Unlike an accountability partner, your peer coach does not have to be in a position to observe you on a regular basis.

Instead, *you* report to him or her on your own progress. A peer coach serves as a mirror who helps hold you accountable to yourself.

Peer coaching works best when peers develop a script, a dual questionnaire that identifies daily actions each wishes to undertake. Because this list changes over time, it is helpful to regularly update it. Questions can deal with the personal and specific—how many sit-ups did you do today?—or with long-term modifications you'd like to make in your behavior—for example, saying yes when you meant to say no. Once the list is in place, peer coaches commit to speak with one another at a specified interval—daily or weekly is usually best. Peers go through their questions quickly without necessarily needing to elaborate or explain. The result can be a speed-dial check-in or a thoughtful exchange.

Here's an example of a few peer coaching questions from someone whose development goal is to try to be more thoughtful and intentional:

Did you create time for yourself to think a problem through?

Were you able to look at something through another person's eyes?

Did you truly listen before jumping in?

Did you pause before you spoke?

Almost nothing is too small to address with a peer coach because behavioral improvements take place in incremental steps. When you work with a peer coach you make a commitment to focus on very specific actions that can help you achieve your vision over time. Doing so enables you to see if your habitual behaviors support or undermine your ability to act upon what you see. Once you've corrected those behaviors, you can move on to something else.

Remain Fully Present

Achieving your vision requires balancing persistence with flexibility, commitment with being open to new ideas. How do you reconcile these seeming contradictions? How do you accommodate long- and short-term concerns? The answer to both these questions is the same. You remain fully present in the moment.

Presence, full participation in whatever is occurring *now*, is difficult to achieve in today's 24/7 environment. Technologies of communication have raised expectations of what we can accomplish and have set a pace that is virtually programmed to exhaust us. A continuing stream of demands makes it difficult for everybody to distinguish what is truly urgent from time-wasting distractions. With each passing year it becomes more difficult—and yet also more essential—to preserve our energy and maintain a mindful balance.

Given their multiple responsibilities and susceptibility to tipping into stress (see the boredom/stress continuum in chapter 5), women in particular must protect their energy and focus if they are to act upon their vision. Three practices can be particularly useful here. We need to set boundaries, avoid multitasking, and learn to let go.

Set Boundaries

Because the nature of today's technologies erodes boundaries in time and space, we must all be highly intentional about setting them for ourselves rather than expecting our organizations to do this for us. Each of us must, in effect, become our own human resources department, implementing policies and practices that support our capacity to be mindful, present, innovative, and thoughtful. Each of us needs to spell out what we can and cannot be responsible for and how we will and will not use our time. If we don't, we will collude in diminishing our own value to our organizations.

Setting boundaries is difficult and cannot be done well in response to pressure. We need to define our parameters *before* we take on a job or project. We must also sell our personal policies to our bosses or managers by articulating how those policies will help us to benefit the organization. To make this work, we must amass sufficient equity and credibility in our job to assure that our parameters will be respected.

Avoid Multitasking

Nothing undermines our ability to be present as much as the compulsion to multitask. Many women regard their capacity to multitask as a badge of honor, yet doing so significantly detracts from being able to function at the level that implementing one's vision requires. Recent scientific studies show that multitasking inhibits creativity and promotes sloppy work.[3] When we make the decision to multitask, we are in essence agreeing to diminish the value of our contribution and erode our long-term viability in our job.

Multitasking also fragments our attention by requiring us to split our mental focus. When our focus is divided, we cannot be fully present to our task, to ourselves, or to others. Being distracted lessens our ability to project authority; we seem fragmented because we *are*. This may be the most pernicious effect of multitasking, especially for women, who must often work consciously to develop a leadership presence. A strong presence requires being fully *present*. Of course, none of us can completely avoid multitasking—it's built into how we live our lives. But we can avoid using it as a default mode, and we need to recognize that dividing our attention will always entail a cost.

Learn to Let Go

Recent studies have documented that women are more apt than men to ruminate, or dwell upon the details of interactions. For example, a UCLA survey revealed that women tend to mull over problems while men are more likely to ignore them, either by turning their attention elsewhere or seeking escape.[4] Rumination may be a consequence of women's capacity to notice the details of human interaction and invest these details with emotional power. It may also be connected with women's tend-and-befriend response, which leads them to talk problems through with friends. This can be an enormously helpful behavior, but carried too far it can develop into a habit of rehashing disappointments, which exacerbates stress and keeps women from acting on what they see.

Rumination is best counteracted through conscious reframing: telling yourself a positive story that plausibly explains a troublesome situation. In psychological terms, to reframe is to reinterpret an event in a way that alters its emotional impact. At the simplest level, this could involve telling yourself that your boss probably yelled at you because he had a fight with his wife that morning. By defusing how his behavior affects you,

you give yourself permission to shift your attention toward more productive channels.

Setting boundaries, avoiding multitasking, and learning to let go are practices that enable you to become more present. Lourine Clark, an accomplished executive coach who works with CEOs, notes that presence is an essential aspect of authenticity.

She says, "We need to speak the truth if we are to have the energy and presence we need to serve others. When we push unpleasant things down, or refuse to acknowledge them, we only harm ourselves. We need to let them surface so we can deal with them while also staying true to the moment. Only by bringing our authentic selves into the light will we have the energy we need to realize what is in our hearts."

If we want to serve as advocates for our own vision, we must protect our energy so we can draw on our authentic capacity for serenity and joy. As Dr. Mary O'Malley (mentioned in chapter 1) points out, the Chinese pictogram for "busyness" juxtaposes the symbol for the heart with the symbol for a dagger. When we allow events to overwhelm us, we undermine both our health and the energy that comes from our hearts. To sheathe the dagger, we must become present to the moment.

CHAPTER EIGHT

Creating the Conditions

W omen must take the lead in asserting the female vision in order for it to have substantive influence in the world. But organizations also need to support women's ability to share their vision by creating conditions that help women integrate the power of what they see into their daily work.

We suggest four organizational practices that can ease the way. Each is subtle but significant, rooted in a shift of awareness about what resources women require and what barriers still undermine their contribution. Unless these changes are instituted, talented women will continue to leave organizations, the leadership pool will remain thin, and major decisions will be made from an arbitrarily narrow base of knowledge. Stand-alone women's initiatives can't turn things around. A cultural transformation is required.

To create the conditions in which women's vision can flourish, organizations must learn to value diverse ways of knowing, encourage mindfulness, support webs of inclusion, and respect the power of empathy. These capacities must be incorporated into the organization's reward structure, compensation policies, and performance reviews as well as into its larger vision.

Value diverse ways of knowing

Organizations need to become more proficient at acknowledging diverse ways of knowing rather than continuing to privilege what can be quantified and empirically supported. We do not mean to suggest that intuitive ways of knowing should be preferred to rational analysis—an inversion of the present practice. Rather, the full spectrum of cognition—the rich complexity of means by which humans come to *know*—must be recognized as having potential value. This requires abandoning the common practice of asking anyone who makes a suggestion to immediately back it up with numbers. Instead, people should be encouraged to share insights that may still be in process or that may contradict expectations.

Even insights that are ultimately discarded can have value by leading to other fresh ideas, whereas overfocusing on numerical models forestalls this. As the example of Blythe Masters at JP Morgan (cited in chapter 4) makes clear, problems arise when an organization continually tries to run the numbers to make a model work instead of stepping outside the problem to consider whether the accepted model or practice applies.

Women's capacity for broad-spectrum as opposed to focused noticing can make them particularly adept at reading signals in the environment and at putting them together in unexpected ways. Companies that recognize this can reap solid benefits. For example, the insurance/reinsurance company Endurance Specialty Holdings asked Catherine Kalaydjian, an executive vice president and member of the executive team, to lead her company's diversity initiative. Cathy had no background in the field—her role was head of claims at the time—but she brought her talent for observation and straight talk to the effort.

The Endurance CEO had also tasked Cathy with devising a fresh way to think about emerging risks. After looking into the highly compartmentalized ways most companies approach diversity, she decided to integrate the two efforts. She created an emerging risk team that itself embodied diversity, and put it to work doing analysis. The cross-divisional effort was exceptional in that it drew on a broad section of employees at various levels and asked them to do strategic thinking.

Cathy's aim was not to turn diversity into an occasion for "programs, posters and slogans," but to embed it in the heart of the organization's understanding of where its future challenges would lie. By seamlessly incorporating diverse thinking into a larger strategic perspective, Cathy provided a new template for addressing major issues. She then demonstrated the fruits of this approach by tapping two members of the group to co-chair the initiative going forward under her sponsorship. She brought several members of the team along to present its findings to the executive team, providing unprecedented exposure for its members.

Approaches such as Cathy's are difficult in organizations that overvalue analytical knowing. In many companies, there is simply no acceptable language in which to express nonlinear thoughts, no way to justify linking diversity with emerging risk. Rigidities of this kind can discourage women and other outsiders from sharing their best thinking and instill in them the habit of second-guessing useful ideas that don't fit the traditional mold.

Subjecting every assertion or suggestion to quantitative analysis also makes it difficult to identify new trends because it forces the focus onto data that reflects the past. Artists have always been ahead of the curve in terms of recognizing what the future will bring precisely because their work derives from inspirations that can at first seem overly subjective. Of course, subjective insights are not always correct, but habitually dismissing what cannot be "proved" by numeric formulae impairs an organization's ability to develop the innovative solutions that a fast-changing global environment demands. Overreliance on numbers frustrates not only women but also those men who would like to bring more intuitive thinking to the table, depriving organizations of a rich vein of potential knowledge.

Encourage Mindfulness

Intuitive skills thrive in an environment where people have sufficient time and space to be mindful. Allowing ideas to surface, germinate, and ripen at their own unforced pace is an inescapable part of the creative process. Mindfulness is also essential if people are to be fully present with one another and for the complexities of the challenges they face. In this way, mindfulness serves collaboration.

But mindfulness is difficult to achieve in frantic organizations that continually pressure their people to push ahead, meet targets, and justify results. In an era when 24/7 technologies have the capacity to raise expectations exponentially, organizations must become better at helping their employees push back against invasive demands. Otherwise, companies risk burning out their best and brightest people, fostering an environment in which habitual busyness becomes addictive and self-defeating.

Addictive busyness also blocks out early warning signals—one reason the financial crisis may have been so widespread.

An overwrought and demanding environment creates particular problems for women. As we saw in chapter 5, women require less stimulation in order to be motivated but can tip more easily into stress. Organizations have traditionally operated on the assumption that people require continual motivation but can handle whatever pressure is thrown their way. This approach is now outdated, because it fails to reflect the needs of a diverse workforce and does not account for how invasive work has become.

All of us today have access to a smorgasbord of tools that enable us to do our work, connect with others, and manage our personal lives. As a result, our work styles have become ever more individual and divergent, more reflective of personal preferences and skills. Yet organizations rarely offer people scope to work in ways that reflect their best talents or to use their time with true efficiency. By insisting on one-size-fits-all policies and practices that are more suited to industrial-era culture, companies inhibit the flexibility that should be one of the great benefits of a diverse workforce.

Incremental policy changes can make a big difference. For example, when working with a professional services firm in Australia, Sally found that the single biggest impediment senior women faced was the firm's system for calculating billable hours. By measuring only quantitative contribution, the organization overlooked significant qualitative improvements that female employees had put in place. By making a few adjustments, the company was able to recalculate its rigid template, significantly improving women's morale and performance.

The strategic planning unit at a U.S. technology firm Sally worked with was able to achieve a similar improvement by granting employees greater latitude in customizing how they used wireless communications. The suggestion had been raised during a women's retreat by several participants who felt that their capacity to think big was being undermined by the requirement that they remain constantly in touch. By reducing the influx of text and employing tools to manage rather than simply respond to information, the women improved functioning, creativity, and morale throughout their unit.

Setting a more mindful tone at the top can also be useful. Enterprises that devalue intuitive thinking also tend to overemphasize the value of action, further fostering addictive busyness. The recent popularity of "execution" as a business buzzword derives from a misplaced perception that leadership is best demonstrated through constant activity. But leadership in a time of uncertainty requires *thoughtful* action based on an understanding of how the future might unfold and what capacities will be needed to address it. Focusing on action for its own sake can cause an individual to miss real opportunities as they arise. It also leads to the perpetually fraught state described by Michele Mayes, general counsel for Allstate, when she said: "A lot of terrible things have happened to me, but most of them never occurred!"

Support Webs of Inclusion

As noted in chapter 5, women thrive on strong relationships, both as a means for coping with stress and as a context in which to process and develop ideas. Simply put, the opportunity to develop high-quality relationships is what makes work *worth it* for many women. Organizations can therefore support women's ability to make strategic contributions by encouraging them to connect broadly and deeply, and by making this an aspect of their (and their bosses') performance review.

Linda Hill, professor of business administration at the Harvard Business School, describes a useful web-building strategy she calls "Development of the Fittest."[1] Noting that traditionally high-potential women were typically given stretch assignments and mentorships, she advocates development plans that include definable and measurable ways of building networks. Hill believes that by articulating the importance of networks as a tool for building women's careers, organizations can legitimize this activity rather than consigning it to informal practice.

Hill recommends recognizing the value of both cohesive and expansive networks. She shows how different kinds of networks help women in different ways. These include improving emotional resilience, allowing the transfer of tacit and implicit knowledge, supporting collaborative endeavors, providing access to new information, conveying political advice, and serving to enhance visibility.

Providing resources to help women connect is good for women, but it is also good for organizations, particularly given that relationships are such a vital tool for retention. For example, when Microsoft gave a group of senior women in one of its business units the time and budget to get together for monthly lunches, two of the women who had been preparing to tender their resignations changed their minds.

Organizations can also encourage women to connect by

putting in place structures that support and reflect how women operate. As Sally found when researching *The Female Advantage*, women tend to be more comfortable putting themselves in the center of things rather than positioning themselves at the top, drawing people in around them and tightening tendrils of connection across boundaries rather than adhering to hierarchical constraints. Carol Gilligan, in her landmark study, *In a Different Voice*, noted that women bond by finding points of connection rather than by establishing where they stand in the pecking order.[2] As a result, women are likely to flourish in inclusive, weblike environments that encourage links across levels. By putting such structures in place at the unit and divisional levels, organizations can support key female strengths while also taking advantage of emerging technologies of communication and social networking.

Respect the Power of Empathy

Empathy is the ability to accurately assess and identify with another person's feelings or point of view. Recent research suggests that empathy operates by means of "mirror neurons" that pick up signals when others speak or show emotion and simulate a corresponding set of feelings in the observer.[3] Several studies show that women have particularly active mirror neuron systems, which may be one reason they are particularly skilled at reading emotional states of others.[4] It is therefore not surprising that women would flourish in organizations where they are able to use their empathic skills.

The capacity for broad-spectrum notice also supports empathy because people are more likely to empathize with what they notice. An environment that values empathy tends to reinforce this essential facet of the female vision. The author and psychiatrist Daniel Siegel calls the capacity for empathic notice "mindsight," which he defines as the ability of the human mind to perceive itself while also perceiving what is in the mind of others.[5] This is a profound advantage in an era in which the borders between our business and our personal lives are eroding.

Julie's early work explored the role of empathy in family systems. Conducting one of the first studies on the subject, she concluded that it takes only a few seconds to determine whether empathy exists between spouses.[6] Because empathy is rooted more in gesture than in words, it is difficult to fake. People know it when they see it. They also feel acutely when empathy is lacking, experiencing it subjectively and at an intuitive level.

Because marriage is one of the most basic of human systems, observations about how couples interact can translate into other relationships. They may have particular resonance for organizations. Empathy can provide concrete benefits in organizations that seek to leverage customer insights, understand the competition, create more effective sales practices, and free the skills of talent development teams.

Since empathy arises from an intuitive understanding both of what others are feeling and how one's own actions affect others, it has far-reaching implications for developing effective leaders. The Center for Creative Leadership's study on self-aware leaders cited in chapter 7 found that empathy thrives on such self-awareness. An empathic individual is not only aware of what someone else is feeling but also of how that experience affects him or her.

Empathy is also an essential resource in managing a diverse workforce. For example, one of Julie's clients had moved from senior management at a large New York publisher to a West Coast online company with a fast-paced youthful culture. She had a hard time at first figuring out how to motivate her sales force, and alternated between being too stern and too friendly. She struggled until she finally recognized the role her *own* reactions played in her back-and-forth with younger workers. In trying to calculate how her suggestions would affect them, she came off as inauthentic. She needed to acknowledge how *she* was feeling and balance that with what she observed; once she made that empathic link, she was able to inspire her team.

An empathic observer not only demonstrates sensitivity but also strength by choosing to acknowledge the pain and confusion that others may feel rather than blocking awareness of these uncomfortable emotions. Empathy requires courage and emotional fortitude. As leadership professor Katherine Bell noted in the *Washington Post*, "Empathizing with your team, your boss, and your coworkers will not make you a pushover but it will make you more powerful."[7] This is why, in Bell's view, empathy has become a critical management skill. She says, "If you can imagine a person's point of view no matter what you think of it, you can more effectively influence the other person."

Lieutenant General William Pagonis, director of the widely hailed logistics command during the first Gulf War, supports this view. As he observed in the *Harvard Business Review*: "Owning the facts is a prerequisite of leadership, but there are millions of technocrats with lots of facts in their quivers yet little leadership potential. In many cases what they are missing is empathy. No one is a leader who cannot first put himself in another person's shoes."[8]

Business consultant Dev Patnaik describes empathic skill as being "wired to care."[9] Patnaik specifically connects empathy to intuition and notes that what people experience in organizations often erodes their capacity for both. We believe that building an empathic organization can be an effective tool not only for improving customer relationships and creativity but also for retaining women.

How do organizations support empathy? They can start by incorporating it as a key leadership capability in performance reviews. Julie's experience suggests that leaders often struggle to provide effective feedback to people in their divisions, teams, and units, in part because they block access to their own emotional reactions. Emphasizing empathic skills could provide a powerful resource for helping leaders deliver feedback in a way that employees can hear and trust.

Organizations can also benefit by training leaders in the concepts of social and cognitive neuroscience, especially the insights gained by identifying how mirror neurons work. Doing so can help leaders increase their perceptiveness about issues of concern to employees, customers, and other stakeholders. This would improve the quality of leadership in the organization while also affirming a key component of the female vision.

From Advantage to Vision

Each of the four practices outlined above can help organizations make better and more strategic use of women's talents. And each can help organizations adapt to the economic, technological, and demographic changes reshaping our future. Incorporating the female vision—its power, its wisdom, its sensitivity, its distinctness—is both desirable and essential in an environment in which every aspect of life is increasingly interconnected and more profoundly social.

In May 1990, Sally published *The Female Advantage: Women's Ways of Leadership*. It was the first book to focus on what women could contribute to organizations instead of how they needed to change and adapt. *The Female Advantage* identified the particular strengths that women bring to organizations— their skill in building relationships, their aptitude for direct communication, their comfort with diversity, their capacity for integrating the different aspects of their lives, their preference for leading from the center rather than the top, their long-term approach to negotiation. The book also showed why these skills were precisely what organizations needed as they moved from an industrial culture based on mass production into an economy in which value is vested in meeting targeted demands.

As the ideas set forth in *The Female Advantage* entered the mainstream, organizations became more comfortable places for women to work. Although many women have felt discouraged by the halting pace of progress since the mid-1990s, the stop-and-start rhythm of change is not surprising when one considers the true scope of what's involved—nothing less than the integration of one half of the human race into every arena of public life.

Looked at from the perspective of several decades, organizations have clearly changed. But they have not changed enough at the leadership level, where the big questions of *why* and *what* are determined. Women fill the ranks but are still under-represented at the top. As a result, their ideas and insights—potentially the most significant gifts they have to offer—have limited impact on the larger environment.

This will not change until organizations begin to recognize the value of what women see as well as the value of what they do. Only then will our workplaces begin to find a harmonious balance, healing our society and enabling it to become more whole. This is inescapable, the next phase of our common human journey.

ACKNOWLEDGMENTS

We have been blessed to have the support of friends, family, clients, and colleagues. Working on this book together was a great adventure, and we both grew a lot along the way.

Thanks to Marshall Goldsmith, the godfather of this book; Linda Basch and her staff at the National Council for Research on Women; Melinda Wolfe for her support and guidance; and the corporate sponsors who enabled us to complete our research project—American Express, Credit Suisse, Deloitte, Goldman Sachs, Lehman Brothers, and Pitney Bowes.

Special thanks go to our research assistant, Anna Henson, for her editorial tenacity and smarts, and to Dr. Mary O'Malley for her clinical expertise in neuroscience. We also thank Rose Snyder for administrative help and Nettie Hartsock for her social networking prowess.

We interviewed and talked through ideas with some of the most distinguished leaders and experts in the United States. Thanks to Liza Bailey, Linda Bialeky, Susan Bird, Sally Blount, Noah Blumenthal, Mary Brabeck, Marjie Calvert, Sandra Cartie, Michelle Clayman, Lynn Connelly, Mike Critelli, Anne Erni, Mary Farrell, Ray Flautt, Diana Grigg, Susan

Harmon, Linda Hill, Juanita James, Barbara Johnson, Don Johnson III, Cathy Kalaydjian, Bev Kaye, Mark Levy, Blythe Masters, Jeanne McGovern, Andrea Nielsen, Dee Pifer, Carol Pledger, Kate Quigley, Janice Reals-Ellig, Amy Starr, Becky Stout, Marion Strauss, Elisabeth Svanberg, Johnna Torsone, Abbie von Schlegell, and Alicia Whitaker.

For technical support we thank Susan Carnes, Steve Kushubar, and John Scott from American Psychological Testing; Dr. Mark Fischman from Carnegie Mellon University; and Michele Salomon at Harris Interactive. Also thanks go to Jim Levine for his advice.

We are grateful to our publisher, Steve Piersanti, whose understanding of our project often surpassed our own, to the staff at Berrett-Koehler for bringing joy and professionalism in equal measure, and to Libba Pinchot, who introduced Sally to Steve.

Each of us had strong personal support to draw on, including our colleagues at The Learning Network. Julie offers thanks to Vicki Brooks, Lourine Clark, Bettina McKee, and Sally Stewart. Sally is grateful first to Elizabeth Bailey, who provided a daily sounding board; and to Marilyn Bethany, Mary Gail Beibel, Michael Keeling, Dianna Garson-White, and as always Bart Gulley.

Both of us are indebted to Doug Reid for his encouragement and support.

NOTES

URLs listed in notes were last accessed February 28, 2010.

PREFACE

1. Herminia Ibarra and Otilia Obodaru, "Women and the Vision Thing," *Harvard Business Review* 87, no. 1 (January 2009), 62–70.

CHAPTER ONE: WHAT WOMEN SEE

1. Mary O'Malley, interview with the authors, December 18, 2009.

2. Katharine McLennan, "The Neuroscience of Leadership and Culture," Mettle Group, March 2007, at www.networkcentral.com.au/documents/NeurosciencesArticle.pdf, 15–16.

3. On diversity of values, see Sally Helgesen and Julie Johnson, *The Satisfaction Profile Assessment*, 2008, published by Harris Interactive, at www.sallyhelgesen.com. See also R. Roosevelt Thomas, *Building on the Promise of Diversity: How We Can Move to the Next Level in Our Workplaces, Our Communities, and Our Society* (New York: AMACOM, 2005), 99–136.

4. On differences in skills between the sexes, see Helen Fisher,

The First Sex: The Natural Talents of Women and How They Are Changing the World (New York: Random House, 1999), 3–29.

5. On how technology is eroding barriers between men and women, work and home, parent and child, teacher and student, see Sally Helgesen, *Everyday Revolutionaries: Working Women and the Transformation of American Life* (New York: Doubleday, 1998), 71–114.

6. O'Malley, interview.

7. On women being unhappy, see Marcus Buckingham, *Find Your Strongest Life* (Nashville: Thomas Nelson, 2009), 29–48. See also responses by Arianna Huffington, "The Sad, Shocking Truth About How Women Are Feeling," *Huffington Post*, September 17, 2009, and Maureen Dowd, "Blue Is the New Black," *New York Times*, September 19, 2009.

8. On the concept of flow, see Mihaly Csikszentmihalyi, *Flow: The Psychology of Optimal Experience* (New York: Harper and Row, 1990), 143–63.

9. O'Malley, interview.

10. Timothy Keller, *Counterfeit Gods: The Empty Promises of Money, Sex and Power, and the Only Hope that Matters* (New York: Dutton Adult, 2009), 74–75.

11. Helgesen and Johnson, *The Satisfaction Profile Assessment*.

CHAPTER TWO: WHY WHAT WOMEN SEE MATTERS

1. Felice Schwartz, "Management Women and the New Facts of Life," *Harvard Business Review* 67, no. 1 (January/February 1989), 65–76.

2. Figures on women in the U.S. workplace from the U.S. Department of Labor, 2009, at www.bls.gov/cps/wlf-databook 2009.html.

3. Sylvia Anne Hewlett and Carolyn Buck Luce, "Off-Ramps and On-Ramps: Keeping Talented Women on the Road to Success," *Harvard Business Review* 83, no. 3 (March 2005), 43–54.

4. Margaret Yap, *The Bottom Line: Connecting Corporate Performance and Gender Diversity*, Catalyst Inc. (2004), at www.catalyst.org/publication/82/the-bottom-line-connecting-corporate-performance-and-gender-diversity, 2.

5. Linda Babcock and Sara Laschever, *Women Don't Ask: Negotiation and the Gender Divide* (New Jersey: Princeton University Press, 2003), 17.

6. Eva Tahmincioglu,. "When Women Rise," *Workforce Management* 83, no. 9 (September 2004), 26–30.

7. Catalyst Inc., *Census of Women Executive Officers and Top Earners of the Fortune 500*, 2009 data available at www.catalyst.org/publication/358/2009-catalyst-census-fortune-500-women-executive-officers-and-top-earners; and www.catalyst.org/publication/357/2009-catalyst-census-fortune-500-women-board-directors.

8. Lisa Belkin, "The Opt-Out Revolution," *New York Times Magazine*, October 26, 2003, at www.nytimes.com/2003/10/26/magazine/the-opt-out-revolution.html.

9. For a description and a debunking of this scenario, see Susan Faludi, *Backlash: The Undeclared War Against American Women* (New York: Crown, 1991), 89–124. The trend Faludi identified continues.

10. On Myra Hart's Harvard Business School study, see Martha Lagace, "Getting Back On Course," *Harvard Business School Working Knowledge*, September 4, 2001, at hbswk.hbs.edu/item/2457.html; and Linda Hirshman, "Homeward Bound," *The American Prospect*, November 21, 2005, at www.prospect.org/cs/articles/articleId=10659.

11. Wanda Wallace, *Reaching the Top: Five Factors that Impact the Retention and Effectiveness of the Most Talented Senior Women*, The Leadership Forum. Major points presented in Wallace's "Executive Summary," at www.lulu.com/content/1018892.

12. Wallace, *Reaching the Top,* "Executive Summary."

13. Steven Pinker, "How the Mind Works," at www.scribd

.com/doc/.../Steven-Pinker-How-the-Mind-Works. See also Susan Pinker, *The Sexual Paradox: Men, Women and the Real Gender Gap* (New York: Scribner,2008), 70.

14. Helgesen and Johnson, *The Satisfaction Profile Assessment.*

CHAPTER THREE: EARLY WARNING SIGNALS

1. On Harvard Business School study, see Lagace, "Getting Back On Course," and Hirshman, "Homeward Bound."

2. Wallace, *Reaching the Top,* "Executive Summary."

3. Michael Lewis, "Wall Street on the Tundra," *Vanity Fair,* April 2009.

4. Sarah O'Connor, "Icelandic Women to Clean Up 'Male Mess'," *Financial Times,* October 13, 2008.

5. Nicholas Khristof, "Mistresses of the Universe," *New York Times,* February 9, 2009, at www.nytimes.com/2009/02/08/opinion/08kristof.html?_r=1.

6. Kevin Sullivan and Mary Jordan, "Rumblings of a Gender Revolution Hit British Banking Industry," *Washington Post,* February 12, 2009.

7. Jason Zweig, *The Little Book of Safe Money* (New York: Wiley, 2009), 157, 164.

8. National Council for Research on Women, Women in Fund Management, 2009. www.ncrw.org/publications.

9. Eric Dash, "Analyst Says Citigroup Needs to Cut Its Dividend," *New York Times,* November 1, 2007.

10. Jon Birger, "The Woman Who Called Wall Street's Meltdown," *Fortune,* August 6, 2008.

11. Sheila Bair, "Fix Rates to Save Loans," *New York Times,* October 17, 2007.

12. Damian Paletta, "FDIC Chief Raps Rescue for Helping Banks Over Homeowners," *Wall Street Journal,* October 16, 2008.

13. Manuel Roig-Franzia, "Credit Crisis Cassandra: Brooksley

Born's Unheeded Warning Is a Rueful Echo Ten Years On," *Washington Post*, May 26, 2009.

14. Peter Goodman, "The Reckoning: Taking Hard New Look at a Greenspan Legacy," *New York Times*, October 8, 2008.

15. Rachel Day, "Federal Officials who Championed Fiscal Responsibility Honored with 2009 JFK Profile in Courage Award," news release, JFK Library Foundation, May 18, 2009, www.jfklibrary.org.

16. Sheila Bair, remarks made upon accepting the 2009 JFK Library Foundation Profile in Courage Award, May 18 2009, at www.jfklibrary.org/Education+and+Public+Programs/Profile+in +Courage+Award.

17. Richard Lacayo and Amanda Ripley, "Persons of the Year 2002: Cynthia Cooper, Colleen Rowley and Sherron Watkins," *Time*, December 30, 2002.

18. Ibid.

19. Sherron Watkins, interview with Sally Helgesen following the 24th Annual Simmons Leadership Conference, April 26, 2003, Boston, MA.

CHAPTER FOUR: BROAD-SPECTRUM NOTICE

1. McLennan, "The Neuroscience of Leadership and Culture," 15–16.

2. Saul Bellow, *The Actual* (New York: Viking, 1997), 15.

3. David Myers, *Psychology*, 8th ed. (New York: Worth Publishers, 2007), 510–13

4. Jason Zweig, *The Little Book of Safe Money*, 159.

5. Susan Bernstein, interview with Sally Helgesen, December 18, 2009.

6. "Intelligence in Men and Women Is a Gray and White Matter," *ScienceDaily*, January 22, 2005, at www.sciencedaily .com/releases/2005/01/050121100142.htm.

7. R. Douglas Fields, "White Matter Matters," *Scientific American* 298, no. 3 (March 2008), 54–61.

8. William Killgore, Mika Oki, and Deborah Yurgelun-Todd, "Sex-Specific Developmental Changes in Amygdala Responses to Affective Faces," *Neuroreport* 12, no. 2 (2001), 427–33, cited in Anne Marie Owens, "Boys' Brains Are from Mars," *National Post*, May 10, 2003.

9. Sue Lovell, interview with Sally Helgesen, July 14, 2009.

10. For more on how webs operate, see Sally Helgesen, *The Web of Inclusion: A New Architecture for Building Great Organizations* (New York: Doubleday, 1995), 19–43.

11. Gillian Tett, *Fool's Gold: How the Bold Dream of a Small Tribe at J. P. Morgan Was Corrupted by Wall Street Greed and Unleashed a Catastrophe* (New York: Free Press, 2009), 251. This is the best book for those who wish to understand the cultural roots of the crisis.

12. Ibid., 140–42.

13. See Sweetman column in Fast Company, www.fast company.com/blog/kate-sweetman/decoding-leadership/ leadership-code-meets-gender-science-part-ii-4-parts. Further details from interview with Julie Johnson, December 30, 2009.

14. Sally Helgesen, *The Female Advantage* (New York: Doubleday, 1990), 29–40.

15. Margaret Heffernan, *How She Does It: How Women Entrepreneurs Are Changing the Rules of Business Success* (New York: Viking Adult, 2007), 70–92. Also published as *Women on Top*.

16. Susan Stewart and others, "Men, Women, and Perceptions of Work Environments, Organizational Commitment, and Turnover Intentions," *Journal of Business and Public Affairs* 1, no. 1 (2007).

17. Jacob Weisberg and Alan Kirschenbaum, "Gender and Turnover: A Re-examination of the Impact of Sex on Intent and Actual Job Changes," *Human Relations* 46, no. 8 (1993), 987–1006.

18. Naomi Eisenberger and Matthew Lieberman, "Why Rejection Hurts: A Common Neural Alarm System for Physical and Social Pain," *Trends in Cognitive Sciences* 8, no. 7 (2004), 294–300.

19. Feng Liu and others on effect of "Activation of Estrogen Receptor Beta," abstract available at www.nature.com/neuro/journal/v11/n3/abs/nn2057.html.

20. Shelley Taylor and others, "Biobehavioral Responses to Stress in Females: Tend-and-befriend, Not Fight-or-flight," *Psychological Review* 107, no. 3 (2000), 411–29.

21. Wanda Wallace, *Reaching the Top*, "Executive Summary."

22. Marshall Goldsmith, interview with the authors, April 12, 2006 and multiple occasions.

23. Daniel Pink, *A Whole New Mind* (New York: Riverhead Books, 2005), 1–3, 52.

CHAPTER FIVE: SATISFACTION DAY BY DAY

1. Helgesen and Johnson, *The Satisfaction Profile Assessment.*

2. Ibid.

3. Dick Grote, "Forced Ranking: Behind the Scenes," *Conference Board Review,* (November/December 2002), at www.conference-board.org/articles/atb_article.cfm?id=146.

4. Louise Story, "Cuomo Says Merrill Deceived Congress on Bonuses," *New York Times*, March 11, 2009.

5. Helgesen and Johnson, *The Satisfaction Profile Assessment.*

6. Helgesen, *The Female Advantage*, 33–35.

7. Henry Mintzberg, *The Nature of Managerial Work* (New York: Harper & Row, 1973), iv–x. See also Helgesen, *The Female Advantage*, 8–14.

8. Helgesen, *The Female Advantage*, 15.

9. Mintzberg, *The Nature of Managerial Work*, Appendix C.

10. David Krasne, "Money for Nothing," *New York Times*, January 27, 2009.

11. Judith Oakley, "Gender-Based Barriers to Senior Management Positions: Understanding the Scarcity of Female CEOs," *Journal of Business Ethics* 27, no. 4 (2000), 321–34.

12. Helgesen and Johnson, *The Satisfaction Profile Assessment*.

13. "Estrogen Makes the Brain More Vulnerable to Stress," *Yale University Medical News*, January 21, 2004, at www.thestressoflife .com/estrogen_makes_the_brain_more_vu.htm.

14. Amy Arnsten, *The Mental Sketchpad: Why Thinking Has Limits*, presentation to the Neuroleadership Summit, New York, October 28, 2008, at www.neuroleadership.org/resources.video .shtml.

15. Ibid.

16. National Women's Business Council, "Women Business Owners and Their Enterprises," fact sheet, July 2007, at www .nwbc.gov/ResearchPublications/keyFacts.html.

17. Heffernan, *How She Does It*, 175–96.

18. Ibid., xi.

19. *The Kauffman Firm Survey: A Comparison of Firms by Gender*, 2009, at www.springerlink.com/index/W74140466363 2884.pdf.

CHAPTER SIX: THE SOCIAL FABRIC

1. "The Pat Heim Series," DVD, February 2009, at www .trainerstoolchest.com/show_product.php?idnum=485.

2. Gordon White, Jr., "Title IX Guidelines Are Issued For Equal Sports Expenditures; Reaction Is Varied Title IX Guidelines Proposed Upgrading Women's Athletics Similar Amounts to Be Spent," *New York Times*, December 7, 1978.

3. Helgesen and Johnson, *The Satisfaction Profile Assessment*.

4. Leonard Greenhalgh, "The Case Against Winning in Negotiation," *Negotiation Journal* 3, no. 2 (April 1987), 171.

5. Helgesen, *The Female Advantage*. 247–50.

6. Sally Helgesen and Marta Williams, "Men and Women: Differing Drivers in the Development of Senior Executive Talent," *CriticalEYE* 14 (Summer 2006).

7. Mike Critelli, interview with Sally Helgesen, November 12, 2009.

CHAPTER SEVEN: ACTING ON YOUR VISION

1. Helgesen and Johnson, *The Satisfaction Profile Assessment*.

2. Jean Leslie, "The Leadership Gap: What You Need, and Don't Have, When It Comes to Leadership Talent," *Center for Creative Leadership*, June 2009, at www.ccl.org/leadership/pdf/research/leadershipGap.pdf.

3. Joanne Silberner, "The Thief of Time: Multitasking Is Inefficient, Studies Show," *NPR Morning Edition*, August 6, 2001, at www.npr.org/programs/morning/features/2001/aug/multitasking/080601multitasking.html.

4. Susan Nolen-Hoeksema, *Sex Differences in Depression* (Stanford, CA: Stanford University Press, 1990), 169. See also Susan Nolen-Hoeksema, "Sex Differences in Unipolar Depression: Evidence and Theory," *Psychological Bulletin* 101, no. 2 (1987), 259–82.

CHAPTER EIGHT: CREATING THE CONDITIONS

1. Linda Hill, "Preparing to Lead," unpublished presentation delivered at Women's Harvard Business School Club of New York, October 12, 2009.

2. Carol Gilligan, *In a Different Voice* (Cambridge: Harvard University Press, 1982), 44–62.

3. Marco Iacoboni and Roger W. McHaney, "Applying Empathy and Mirror Neuron Concepts to NeuroLeadership," *Neuroleadership Journal* 2, (2009), 35–41.

4. Ya-Wei Cheng and others, "Gender Differences in the Human Mirror System: A Magnetoencephalography Study," *NeuroReport*, 17, no. 11 (July 2006), 1115–19.

5. Daniel J. Siegel, *Mindsight: The New Science of Personal Transformation*. (New York: Bantam, 2010), 1–14.

6. Julie Johnson, "Empathic Ability and Adjustment in Marriage," unpublished masters thesis for Southern Methodist University, Dallas, TX, April 23, 1974, presented at the National Association of Marriage and Family, Saint Louis, MO, June 1974.

7. Katherine Bell, "Empathy: Not Such a Soft Skill," *Washington Post*, May 29, 2009.

8. William Pagonis, "Leadership in a Combat Zone," *Harvard Business Review* 79, no. 11 (December 2001), 109–10.

9. Dev Patnaik and Peter Morgensen, *Wired to Care: How Companies Prosper When They Create Widespread Empathy*, (New Jersey: FT Press, 2009), 6–14.

INDEX

SALLY HELGESEN

SALLY HELGESEN is one of the world's brand name experts in the field of women's leadership and the author of five highly influential books. Her best-selling *The Female Advantage: Women's Ways of Leadership,* widely hailed as "the classic work" on what women have to contribute to organizations, has been continuously in print for 20 years, was translated into 11 languages, and is used in colleges and universities around the world. She is also author of *The Web of Inclusion: A New Architecture for Building Great Organizations,* cited in the *Wall Street Journal* as one of the best books on leadership ever published.

Sally delivers keynotes and develops leadership programs for corporations, partnership firms, universities, and non-profits around the world. She has consulted with the United Nations Development Program on building more inclusive and decentralized country offices and strengthening women's programs in Africa and Asia. She has led seminars at the Harvard Graduate School of Education and Smith College, and has been a visiting scholar at Northwestern University and Lauriston Institute in Melbourne, Australia.

Articles about Sally's work have been featured in *Fortune,* the *New York Times,* and *Business Week,* and she has appeared on hundreds of television and radio shows. She is a contributing editor to the magazine *Strategy+Business* and is a member of the New York Women's Forum.

JULIE JOHNSON

JULIE JOHNSON, a graduate of the Harvard Business School, is considered one of the pioneers in the field of executive coaching and has coached hundreds of senior executives in blue chip global organizations. In her work with many of the most successful women in the Fortune 500, Julie has both experienced and helped clients to confront the issues described in *The Female Vision*.

Prior to establishing her leadership coaching practice in 1995, Julie was Vice President of Executive Education at Merrill Lynch, Assistant VP of Human Resource Planning at General Foods, and Director of Recruiting at Vinson and Elkins. She began her career as Director of Placement at Stanford Law School.

Julie's work has been published in the *Harvard Business Review* and featured in the groundbreaking book, *Coaching for Leadership.* She has presented her ideas at the Harvard Business School, Yale School of Management, the Conference Board, and before a range of industry groups. In addition to her MBA from Harvard, Julie holds an MA in Social Psychology and Counseling from Southern Methodist University and a BA from Carnegie Mellon. She is a member of the Advisory Council for the Coaching Coalition and also a member of the International Women's Forum.

Berrett–Koehler
BK Publishers

Berrett-Koehler is an independent publisher dedicated to an ambitious mission: *connecting people and ideas to create a world that works for all*.

We believe that to truly create a better world, action is needed at all levels—individual, organizational, and societal. At the individual level, our publications help people align their lives with their values and with their aspirations for a better world. At the organizational level, our publications promote progressive leadership and management practices, socially responsible approaches to business, and humane and effective organizations. At the societal level, our publications advance social and economic justice, shared prosperity, sustainability, and new solutions to national and global issues.

A major theme of our publications is "Opening Up New Space." Berrett-Koehler titles challenge conventional thinking, introduce new ideas, and foster positive change. Their common quest is changing the underlying beliefs, mindsets, institutions, and structures that keep generating the same cycles of problems, no matter who our leaders are or what improvement programs we adopt.

We strive to practice what we preach—to operate our publishing company in line with the ideas in our books. At the core of our approach is stewardship, which we define as a deep sense of responsibility to administer the company for the benefit of all of our "stakeholder" groups: authors, customers, employees, investors, service providers, and the communities and environment around us.

We are grateful to the thousands of readers, authors, and other friends of the company who consider themselves to be part of the "BK Community." We hope that you, too, will join us in our mission.

A BK Life Book

This book is part of our BK Life series. BK Life books change people's lives. They help individuals improve their lives in ways that are beneficial for the families, organizations, communities, nations, and world in which they live and work. To find out more, visit **www.bk-life.com**.

Berrett–Koehler
Publishers

Connecting people and ideas
to create a world that works for all

Dear Reader,

Thank you for picking up this book and joining our worldwide community of Berrett-Koehler readers. We share ideas that bring positive change into people's lives, organizations, and society.

To welcome you, we'd like to offer you a free e-book. You can pick from among twelve of our bestselling books by entering the promotional code **BKP92E** here: http://www.bkconnection.com/welcome.

When you claim your free e-book, we'll also send you a copy of our e-newsletter, the *BK Communiqué*. Although you're free to unsubscribe, there are many benefits to sticking around. In every issue of our newsletter you'll find

- A free e-book
- Tips from famous authors
- Discounts on spotlight titles
- Hilarious insider publishing news
- A chance to win a prize for answering a riddle

Best of all, our readers tell us, "Your newsletter is the only one I actually read." So claim your gift today, and please stay in touch!

Sincerely,

Charlotte Ashlock
Steward of the BK Website

Questions? Comments? Contact me at bkcommunity@bkpub.com.